PIANO | VOCAL | GUITAR

EDM SHEET MUSIC COLLECTION

37 ELECTRONIC DANCE MUSIC HITS

ISBN 978-1-5400-3319-2

Visit Hal Leonard Online at
www.halleonard.com

Contact Us:
Hal Leonard
7777 West Bluemound Road
Milwaukee, WI 53213
Email: info@halleonard.com

In Europe contact:
Hal Leonard Europe Limited
42 Wigmore Street
Marylebone, London, W1U 2RN
Email: info@halleonardeurope.com

In Australia contact:
Hal Leonard Australia Pty. Ltd.
4 Lentara Court
Cheltenham, Victoria, 3192 Australia
Email: info@halleonard.com.au

CONTENTS

APPLAUSE

Words and Music by STEFANI GERMANOTTA,
PAUL BLAIR, STEVE GUESS,
NICHOLAS MONSON, DINO ZISIS,
WILLIAM GRIGAHCINE, JULIEN ARIAS
and NICHOLAS MERCIER

F Eb F Gm
To crash the crit - ic say - ing, "Is it right or is it wrong?"
I guess, sir, if you say so, some of us just like to read.
F Eb
If on - ly fame had an I -
One sec - ond I'm a Koons, then
Cm F Gm F Eb
V, ba - by, could I bear be - ing a -
sud - den - ly the Koons is me. Pop cul - ture
Cm F Gm
way from you. I found the vein, put it in here.
was an art, now art's a pop cul - ture in me.
I live for the ap -

Gm
F
E♭
Cm
F
Gm
3fr
plause, ap-plause, ap - plause. I live for the ap - plause, plause. Live for the ap -
F
E♭
plause, plause. Live for the way that you cheer and scream for me. The ap -
Cm
F
Gm
F
E♭
plause, ap-plause, ap - plause. Give me that thing that I love,
Cm
F
Gm
I'll turn the lights on. Put your hands up, make 'em touch. Make it real loud.

F
E♭
Cm
F
Gm
Give me that thing that I love, I'll turn the lights on.
Put your hands up, make 'em touch.
Make it real loud.
A - P - P - L - A - U - S - E.
Make it real loud.
Cm
F
Gm
F
E♭
Put your hands up, make 'em touch, touch.
A - P - P - L - A - U -
- S - E.
Make it real loud.
To Coda
1
Cm
F
Gm
Put your hands up, make 'em touch, touch.

2
Cm
F
Gm
F
E♭
Put your hands up, make 'em touch, touch. Ooh, touch,
touch, ooh, touch, touch, ooh, ooh,
ooh, ooh. I live for the ap -
N.C.
D.S. al Coda
CODA
Put your hands up, make 'em touch, touch. A - R - T - P - O - P.

CLOSER

Words and Music by ANDREW TAGGART,
FREDERIC KENNETT, ISAAC SLADE,
JOSEPH KING, ASHLEY FRANGIPANE
and SHAUN FRANK

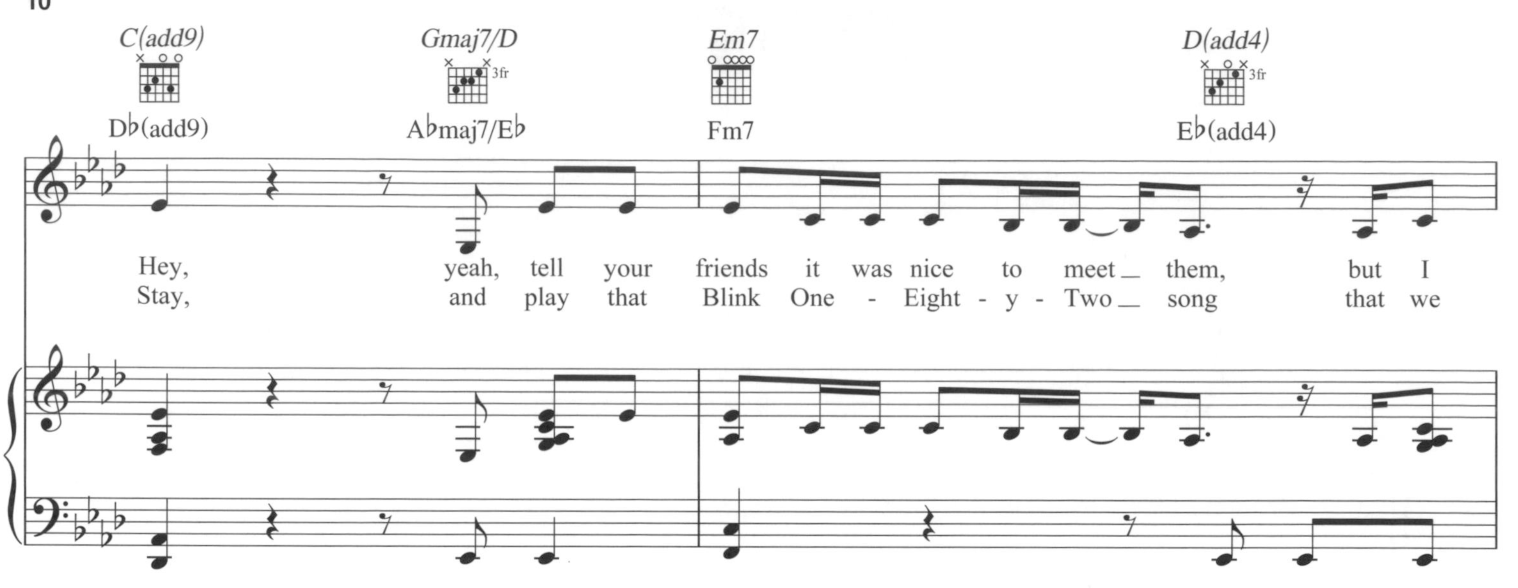
C(add9)
Gmaj7/D
Em7
D(add4)
3fr
Db(add9)
Abmaj7/Eb
Fm7
Eb(add4)
Hey, yeah, tell your friends it was nice to meet them, but I
Stay, and play that Blink One - Eight - y - Two song that we

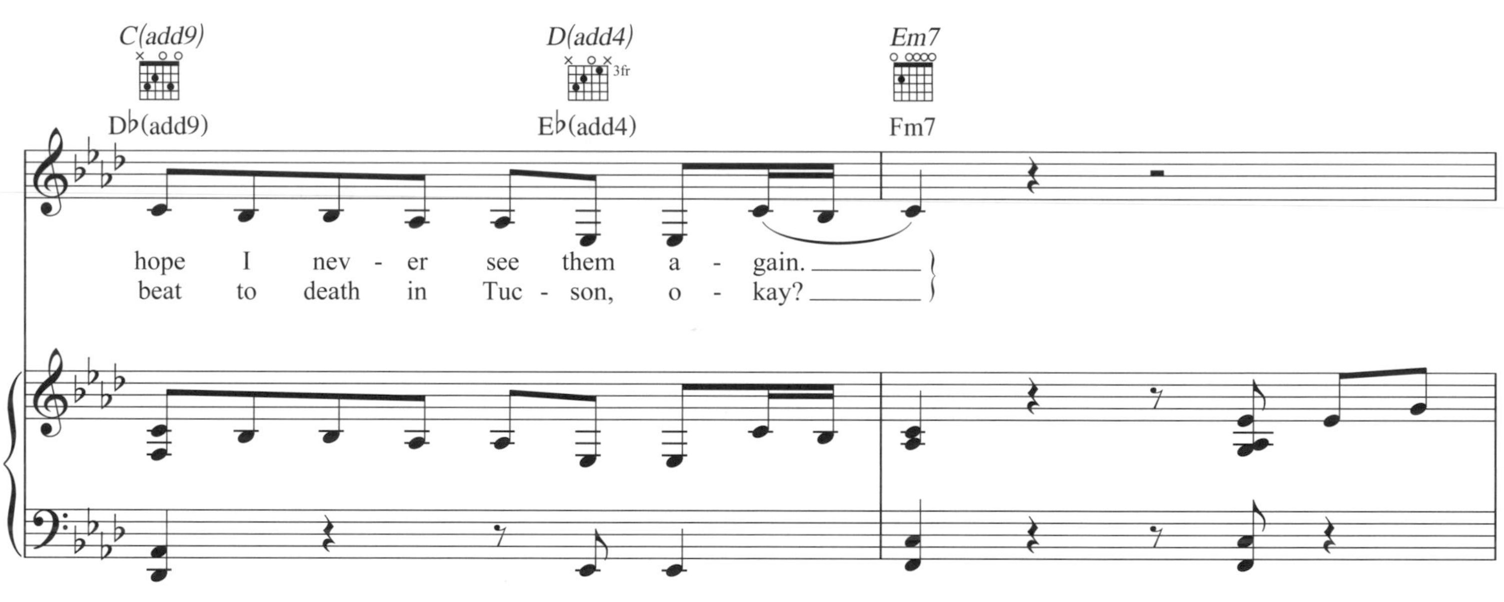
C(add9)
D(add4)
Em7
3fr
Db(add9)
Eb(add4)
Fm7
hope I nev - er see them a - gain.
beat to death in Tuc - son, o - kay?

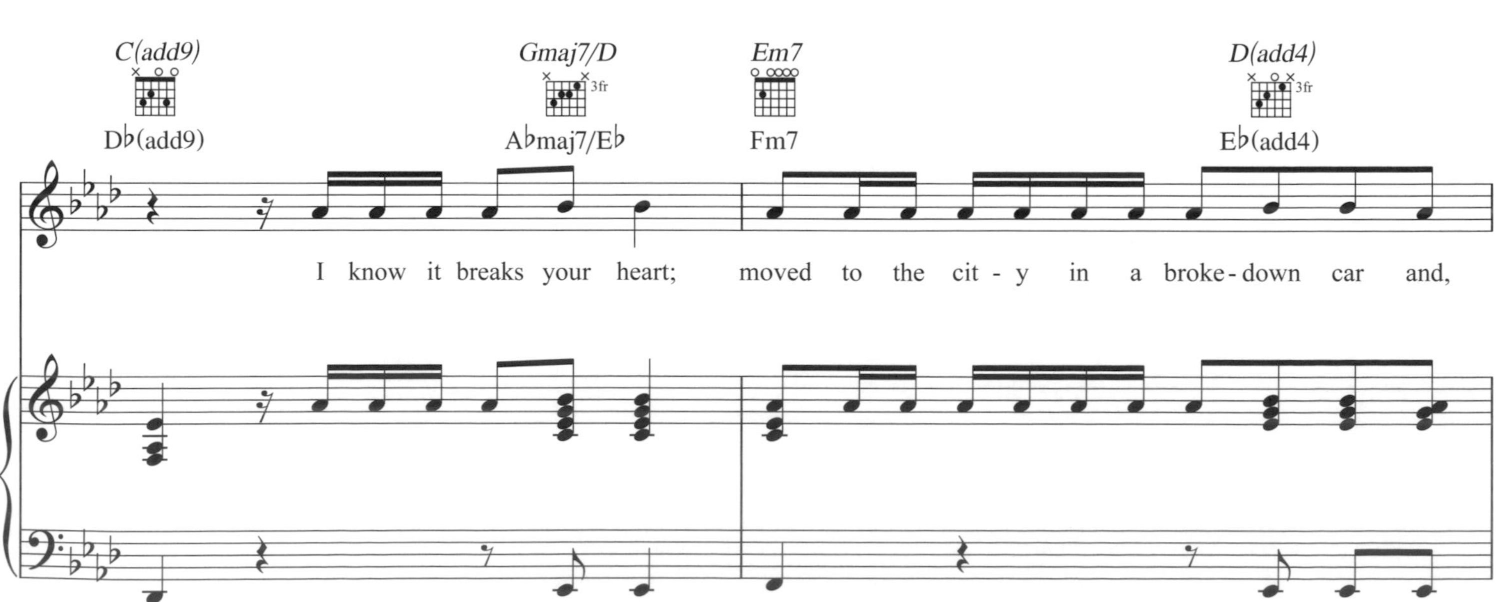
C(add9)
Gmaj7/D
Em7
D(add4)
3fr
Db(add9)
Abmaj7/Eb
Fm7
Eb(add4)
I know it breaks your heart; moved to the cit - y in a broke - down car and,

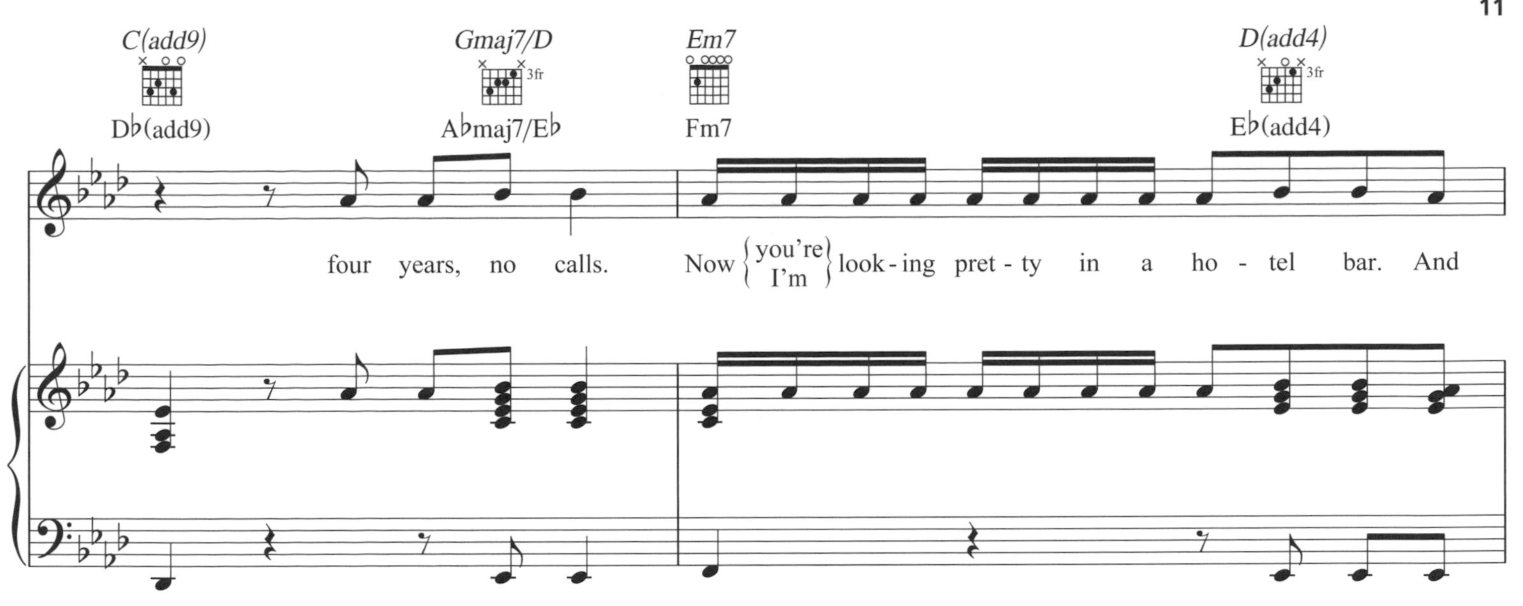
C(add9)
Gmaj7/D
Em7
D(add4)
3fr
D♭(add9)
A♭maj7/E♭
Fm7
E♭(add4)
four years, no calls. Now {you're / I'm} look-ing pret-ty in a ho-tel bar. And

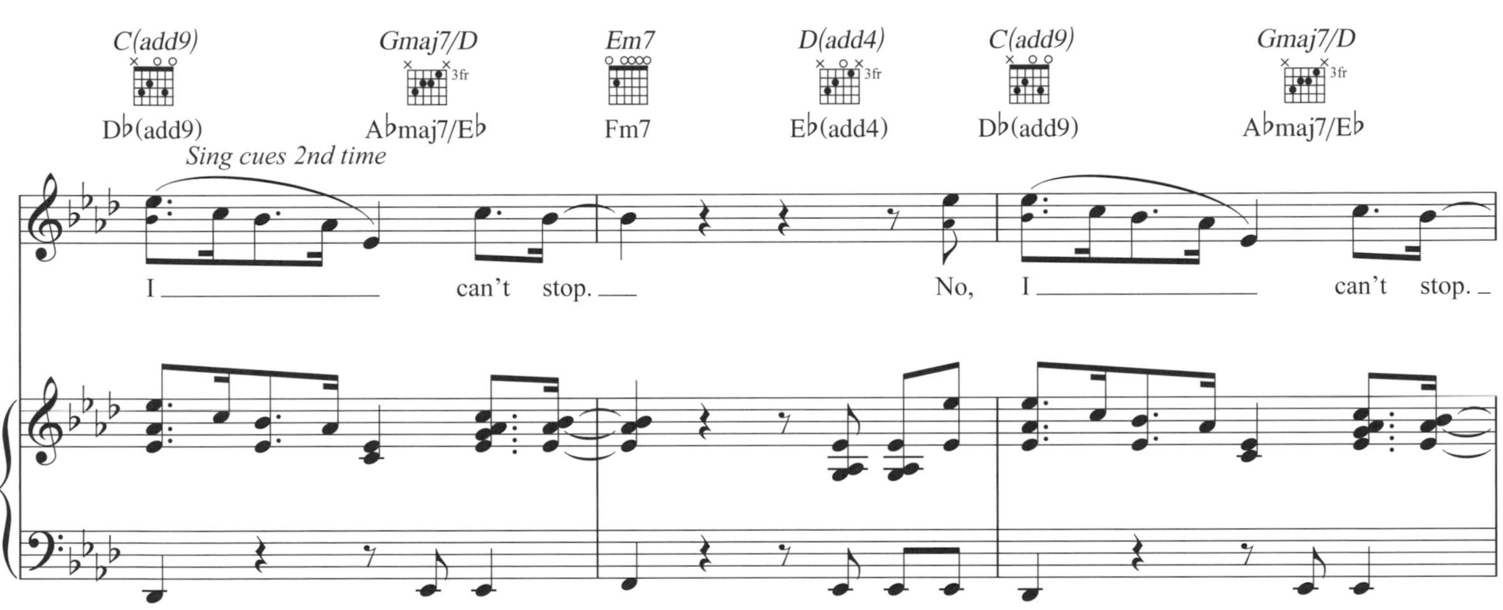
C(add9)
Gmaj7/D
Em7
D(add4)
C(add9)
Gmaj7/D
3fr
D♭(add9)
A♭maj7/E♭
Fm7
E♭(add4)
D♭(add9)
A♭maj7/E♭
Sing cues 2nd time
I can't stop. No, I can't stop.

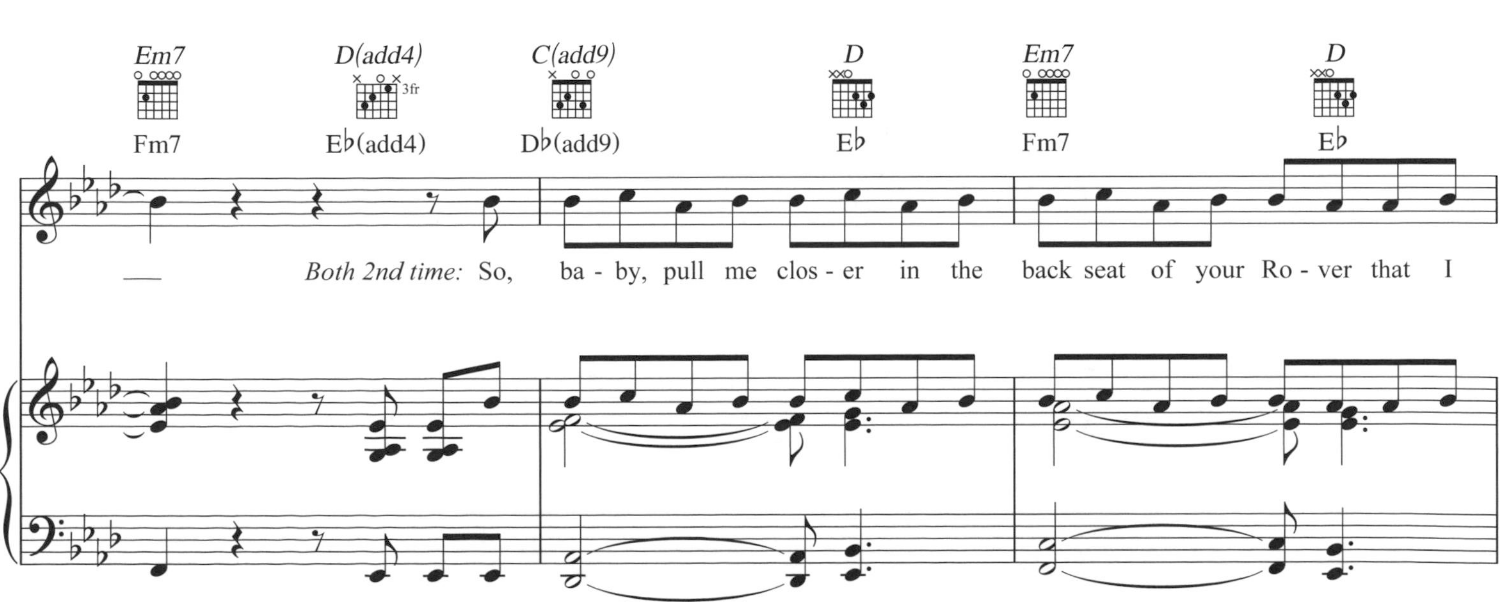
Em7
D(add4)
C(add9)
D
Em7
D
3fr
Fm7
E♭(add4)
D♭(add9)
E♭
Fm7
E♭
Both 2nd time: So, ba-by, pull me clos-er in the back seat of your Ro-ver that I

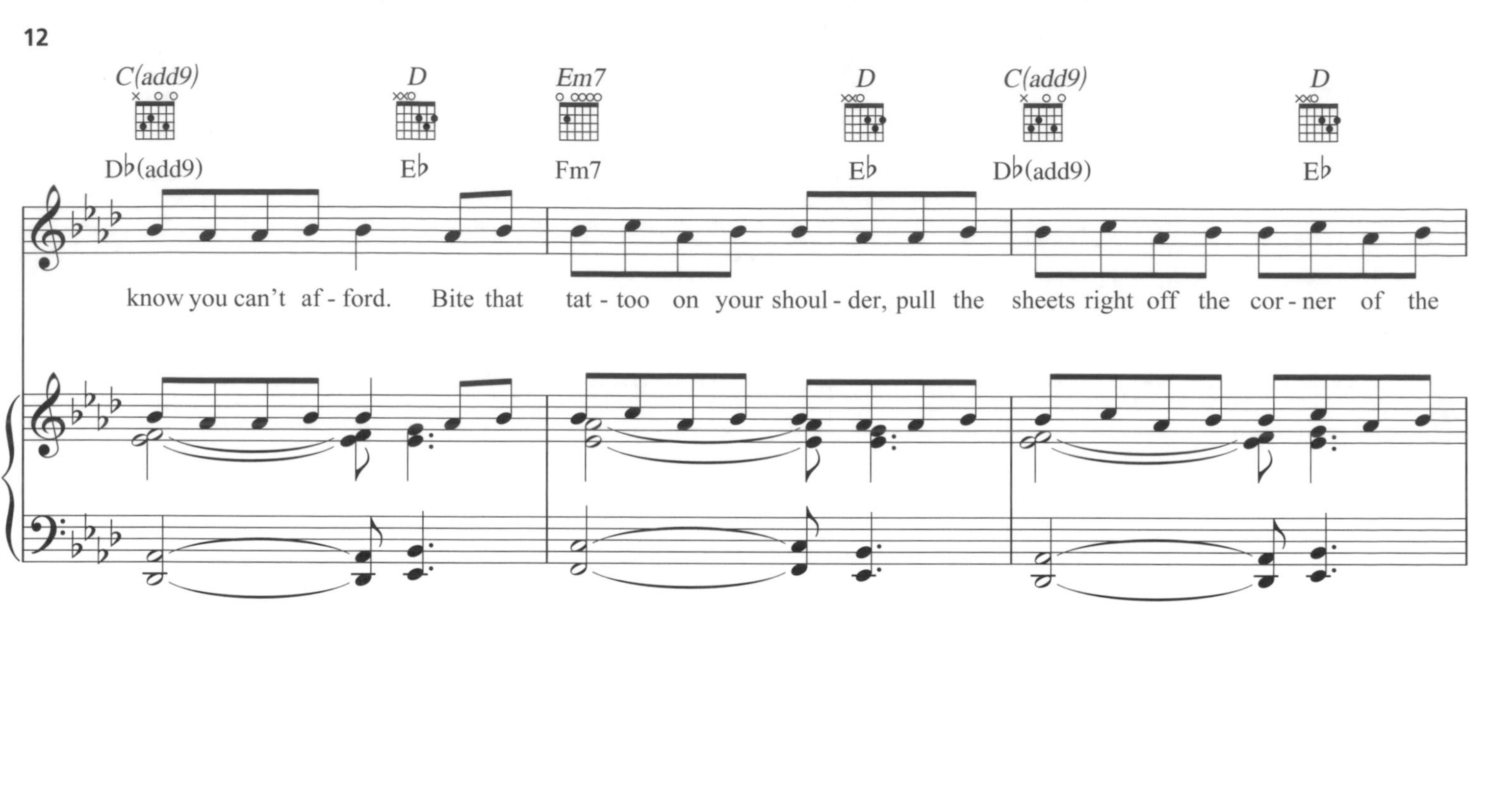
C(add9)
D
Em7
D
C(add9)
D
D♭(add9)
E♭
Fm7
E♭
D♭(add9)
E♭
know you can't af - ford. Bite that tat - too on your shoul - der, pull the sheets right off the cor - ner of the

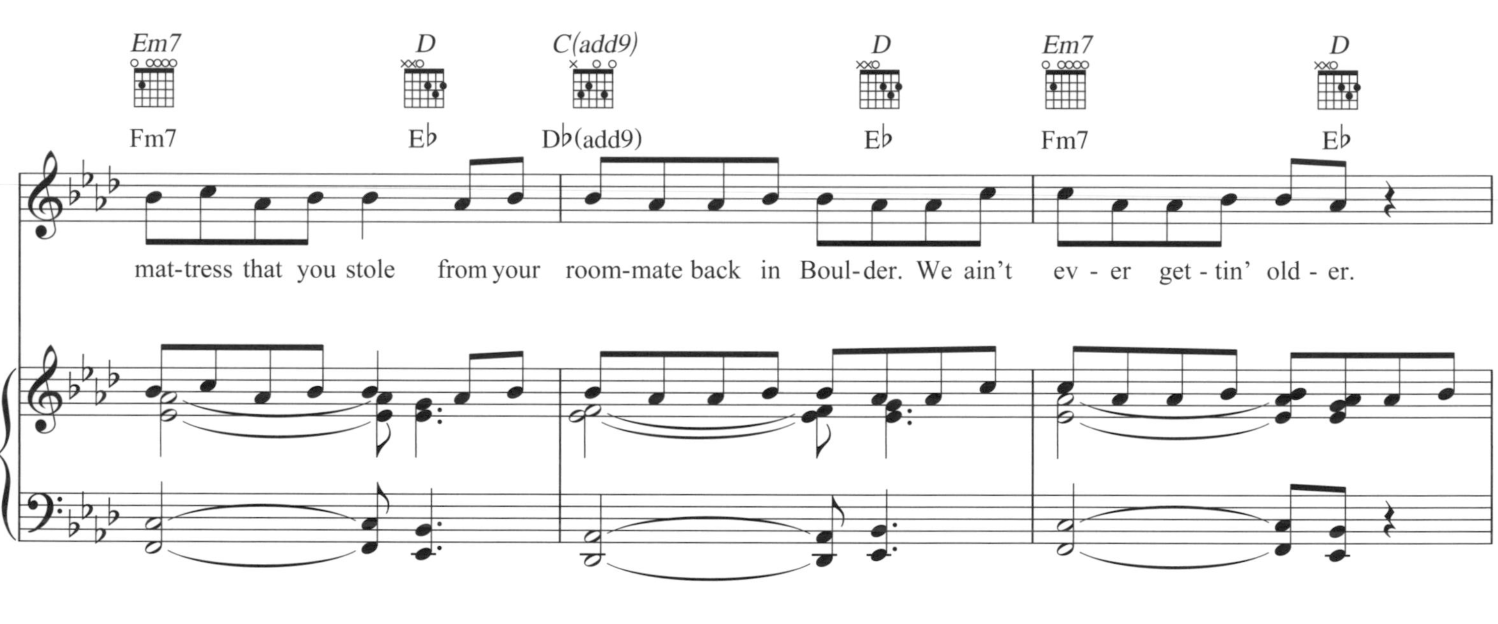
Em7
D
C(add9)
D
Em7
D
Fm7
E♭
D♭(add9)
E♭
Fm7
E♭
mat-tress that you stole from your room-mate back in Boul-der. We ain't ev - er get - tin' old - er.

C(add9)
Gmaj7/D
Em7
D(add4)
C(add9)
Gmaj7/D
3fr
D♭(add9)
A♭maj7/E♭
Fm7
E♭(add4)
D♭(add9)
A♭maj7/E♭
We ain't

Em7
D
C(add9)
Gmaj7/D
Em7
D(add4)
Fm7
E♭
D♭(add9)
A♭maj7/E♭
Fm7
E♭(add4)
ev - er get - tin' old - er.
C(add9)
Gmaj7/D
1
Em7
D
2
Em7
D
D♭(add9)
A♭maj7/E♭
Fm7
E♭
Fm7
E♭
We ain't ev - er get - tin' old - er.
ev - er get - tin' old - er.
Male:
So,
C(add9)
D
Em7
D
C(add9)
D
D♭(add9)
E♭
Fm7
E♭
D♭(add9)
E♭
ba - by, pull me clos - er in the back seat of your Ro - ver that I know you can't af - ford. Bite that

Em7
D
C(add9)
D
Em7
D
Fm7
E♭
D♭(add9)
E♭
Fm7
E♭
tat - too on your shoul - der, pull the sheets right off the cor - ner of the mat - tress that you stole from your
C(add9)
D
Em7
D
C(add9)
D
D♭(add9)
E♭
Fm7
E♭
D♭(add9)
E♭
room - mate back in Boul - der. We ain't ev - er get - tin' old - er. We ain't ev - er get - tin' old - er. We ain't
Female: We ain't
Em7
D
C(add9)
D
1
Em7
D
Fm7
E♭
D♭(add9)
E♭
Fm7
E♭
ev - er get - tin' old - er. We ain't ev - er get - tin' old - er. We ain't ev - er get - tin' old - er. We ain't
ev - er get - tin' old - er. Female: No, we ain't ev - er get - tin' old - er.

2
Em7
C(add9)
Gmaj7/D
D(add4)
3fr
Fm7
N.C.
D♭(add9)
A♭maj7/E♭
E♭(add4)
ev - er get - tin' old - er.
ev - er get - tin' old - er.
Both: We ain't ev - er get - tin' old - er.
No, we ain't ev - er get - tin' old - er.
D
E♭

BEAUTIFUL NOW

Words and Music by ANTONINA ARMATO,
TIMOTHY PRICE, ANTON ZASLAVSKI,
JONATHAN BELLION, DESMOND CHILD
and DAVID JOST

A
F♯m
Gmaj7
A
it? We're beau - ti - ful now.
We're beau - ti - ful now.
Bm
Em
G
We might not know why,
we might not know how,
D
Bm7
F♯m
but, ba - by, to - night
we're beau - ti - ful now.
We'll light up the sky,
G
D
A
Bm7
we'll o - pen the clouds
'cause, ba - by, to - night
we're beau - ti - ful now.

F♯m
G
D
We're beau - ti - ful. Ba, ba, ba, ba, ba, ba, ba, ba, ba, ba,
Bm7
F♯m
G
ba, ba, ba, ba, ba, ba, ba, ba, ba, ba, ba. Ba, ba, ba, ba, ba,
D
A
Bm7
F♯m
N.C.
ba, ba, ba, ba, ba, ba, ba, ba, ba, ba, ba, ba, we're beau - ti - ful.
G
D
Bm7
Ba, ba, ba, ba, ba, ba, ba, ba, ba, ba, ba, ba, ba, ba,

F♯m
G
D
A
ba, ba, ba, ba, ba, ba, ba. Ba, ba, ba, ba, ba, ba, ba, ba, ba, ba,
Bm7
1 F♯m
2 F♯m
N.C.
ba, ba, ba, ba, ba, ba, ba. Wher-ev-er it's go-
ba, ba, ba, ba, ba, ba, ba.
G
D
Bm7
F♯m
Ba, ba, ba, ba, ba, ba, ba, ba, ba, ba, ba, ba, ba, ba, ba, ba, ba, ba, ba, ba, ba.
G
D
A
Bm7
F♯m
Ba, ba, ba, ba, ba, ba, ba, ba, ba, ba, ba, ba, ba, ba, ba, ba, ba, ba, ba, ba, ba.

G
D
Bm7
F♯m
Let's live to-night like fire - flies, and one by one light up the sky.
G
D
A
Bm7
We dis - ap - pear and pass the crown. You're beau - ti - ful, you're
A/C♯
G
D
beau - ti - ful, you're beau - ti - ful now. You're beau - ti - ful now.
Bm
F♯m
G
You're beau - ti - ful now.

D
A
Bm
F♯m
N.C.
You're beau - ti - ful now.
We're beau - ti - ful.
G
D
Bm7
Ba, ba, ba, ba, ba, ba, ba, ba, ba, ba, ba, ba, ba, ba,
F♯m
G
D
A
ba, ba, ba, ba, ba, ba, ba. Ba, ba, ba, ba, ba, ba, ba, ba, ba, ba,
Bm7
1
F♯m
N.C.
2
F♯m
ba, ba, ba, ba, ba, ba, ba, ba, ba, ba, ba. ba, ba, ba, we're beau - ti - ful.

BREAK FREE

Words and Music by SAVAN KOTECHA,
MAX MARTIN and ANTON ZASLAVSKI

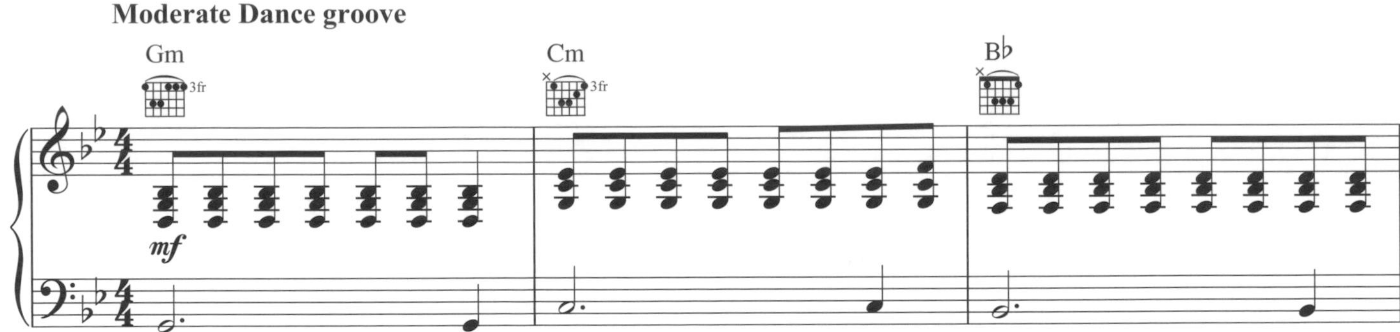

Cm
3fr
B♭
E♭
3fr
fake it. I can't pre-tend an-y-more, ooh.
fe-ver, yeah, babe, on the high-way to hell, ooh.
Gm
3fr
Cm
3fr
B♭
I on-ly wan-na die a-live, nev-er by the hands of a
E♭
3fr
Gm
3fr
Cm
3fr
bro-ken heart, ooh. I don't wan-na hear you lie to-night, now
B♭
D
E♭
3fr
that I've be-come who I real-ly am. This is

Gm F B♭/D E♭ Gm F B♭
the part when I say I don't want ya. I'm strong-er than I've been be-fore.
E♭ Gm F B♭/D E♭
This is the part when I break free 'cause
Cm7 B♭/D E♭ Gm F B♭/D
I can't re-sist it no more. This is the part when I
E♭ Gm F B♭ E♭
say I don't want ya. I'm strong-er than I've been be-fore. This is

Gm
F
B♭/D
E♭
3fr
To Coda
the part when I break free 'cause I can't re - sist it no
1
more.
You were
2
Cm7
B♭/D
E♭
F
more.
No more, ba -
Gm
Dm7
Cm7
B♭/D
by,
ooh.

E♭ F Gm Dm7
Thought on your bod - y I came a - live;
Cm7 B♭/D E♭ F Gm
it was le - thal, it was fa - tal. In my dreams
Dm7 Cm7 B♭/D E♭ F
it felt so right, but I woke up ev - 'ry time.
Gm F B♭

E♭
3fr
D.S. al Coda
CODA
N.C.
Ooh, ba - by, this is
I can't re - sist it no
G5
3fr
more.
Gm
3fr

COLD WATER

Words and Music by THOMAS PENTZ,
KAREN ØRSTED, HENRY ALLEN,
PHILIP MECKSEPER, JUSTIN BIEBER,
BENJAMIN LEVIN, ED SHEERAN
and JAMIE SCOTT

C♯m D F♯m A
Oh.
You should-n't be drown - ing on your own.
You should-n't be fight - ing on your own.
C♯m D F♯m A C♯m D
And if you feel you're sink-ing, I will jump right o-ver in-to
F♯m A C♯m D F♯m A
cold, cold wa-ter for you. And al-though time may take us in-to
C♯m D F♯m A C♯m D
dif-fer-ent plac-es, I will still be pa-tient with you. And I want you to

E5 N.C. F♯m A C♯m D

know, I won't let go. I'll be your

F♯m A C♯m D

life - line to - night. I won't let

F♯m A C♯m D

go. I'll be your

F♯m A 1 C♯m D 2 C♯m D

life - line to - night.

F♯m7
A(add2)
C♯m7
4fr
Dsus2
Female:
Come on, come on, save me from my rock - ing boat. I just wan - na stay a -
float. I'm all a - lone. And
I hope, I hope some - one's gon - na take me home, some - where I can rest my
soul. I need to know you won't let go.
N.C.
F♯m
A

C♯m D F♯m A
4fr
Male: I'll be your life - line to - night.
C♯m D F♯m A C♯m D
Female: You won't let go. Male: I'll be your
F♯m A C♯m D F♯m A
life - line to - night. I won't let go.
C♯m D F♯m A C♯m
N.C.
I won't let go.

DON'T LET ME DOWN

Words and Music by ANDREW TAGGART,
EMILY SCHWARTZ and SCOTT HARRIS

* Recorded a half step lower.

G
Am
F
Strand - ed,
Run - ning
C
G
Am
reach - ing out.
out of time,
I call your name, but you're not a - round.
I real - ly thought you were on my side.
F
C
I say your name, but you're not a - round.
But now there's no - bod - y by my side.
G
Am
I

F
C
G
need you, I need you, I need you right now.
Yeah, I need you right
Am
F
C
now.
So don't let me, don't let me, don't let me down.
G
Am
F
I think I'm los - ing my mind, now.
It's in my head, dar - ling, I
C
G
Am
hope that you'll be here when I need you the most.
So

To Coda
F
C
G
don't let me, don't let me, don't let me down.
D - don't let me
Am
N.C.
A5
down, don't let me down.
A5/G
A5
Don't let me down, down, down.
1
A5/G
Don't let me down, don't let me down, down, down.

2
A5/G
Don't let me down, down, down.
A5
Don't let me
A5/G
A5
down, down, down.
Don't let me
A5/G
F
down, don't let me down, down, down.

C
G
Ooh, I think I'm los - ing my mind,
Am
F
C
now, yeah. Ooh,
G
Am
D.S. al Coda
I think I'm los - ing my mind, now, yeah. I
CODA
G
Am
N.C.
Don't let me down.

F
C
G
Vocal ad lib. on repeats
Yeah - eah, don't let me
1–3
Am
4
Am
F
down.
Don't let me down.
C
G
Am
Don't let me down, down, down.
F
C
G
Am

FADED

Words and Music by ALAN WALKER,
ANDERS FRØEN, GUNNAR GREVE
and JESPER BORGEN

* Recorded a half step higher.

Dm
Bb
F
now?
Where are you now?
C
Dm
Bb
Where are you now?
Was it all in my fan - ta - sy?
Where are you
F
C
N.C.
now?
Were you on - ly i - mag - i - nar - y?
Where are you
Dm
Bb
now?
At - lan - tis, un - der the sea,

F
C
under the sea.
Where are you
Dm
B♭
now?
Another dream;
the
F
C
monster's running wild inside of me.
I'm fad - ed.
Dm
B♭
I'm fad - ed.

F
C
So lost, I'm fad - ed.
Dm
B♭
F
To Coda
I'm fad - ed.
So
C
Dm
B♭
lost, I'm fad - ed. These shal-low wa-ters nev - er met what I need-ed;
F
C
Dm
I'm let - ting go, a deep-er dive. E - ter - nal si-lence of the

B♭
F
C
sea; I'm breath - ing, a - live. Where are you
Dm
B♭
F
now? Where are you now?
C
Dm
Un - der the bright but fad - ed lights, you've set my heart
B♭
F
C
on fi - re. Where are you now? Where are you now?
Vocal effects ad lib.

Dm
B♭
F
C
Vocal effects end
N.C.
D.S. al Coda
Where are you
CODA
C
lost, I'm fad - ed.
Dm
B♭
F
C
rit.

FEEL THIS MOMENT

Words and Music by ARMANDO PEREZ, PAL WAAKTAAR,
MORTEN HARKET, CHRISTINA AGUILERA, MAGNE FURUHOLMEN,
NASRI ATWEH, ADAM MESSINGER, URALES VARGAS
and NOLAN LAMBROZZA

D G C G/B
is glow - in', I'll be in my cas - tle gold - en.
Am D G
But un - til the gates are o - pen, I just wan - na feel
C G/B Am D
this mo - ment. Whoa,
G C G/B Am
I just wan - na feel this mo - ment. Whoa,

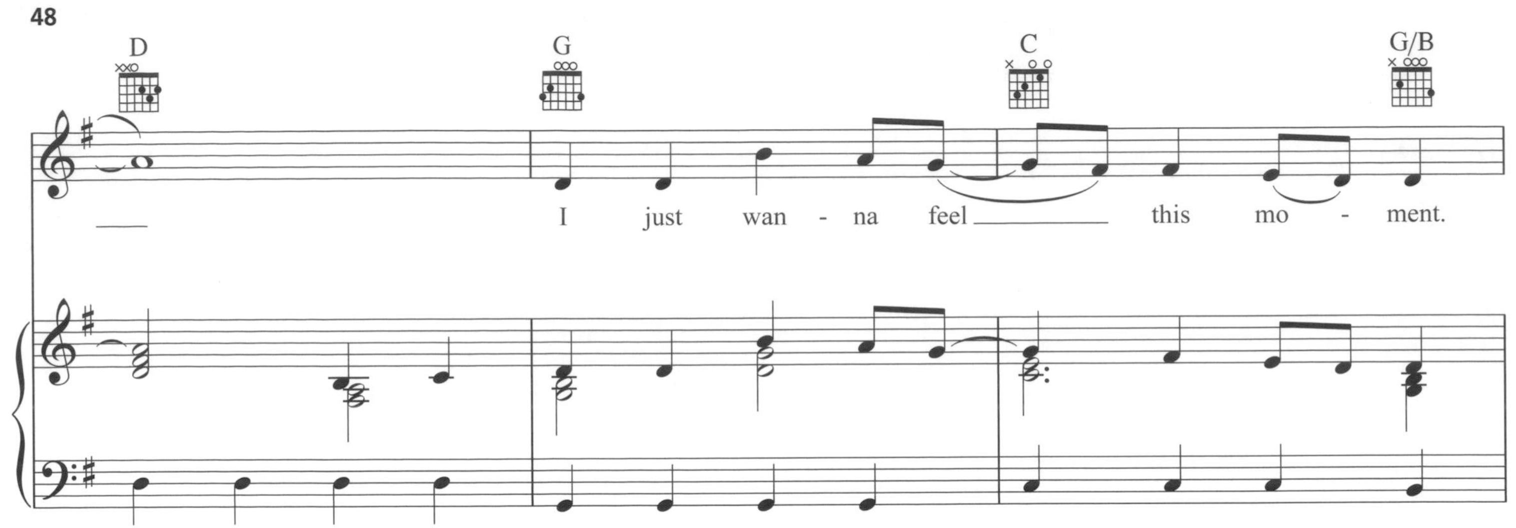
D
G
C
G/B
I just wan - na feel this mo - ment.

N.C.

Am
I just wan - na feel this mo - ment.

D
G
C
G/B
Am
D
G
C
N.C.
Am
D
Feel this mo - ment.
Rap 1: (See additional lyrics)
Rap 2: (See additional lyrics)
G
C
G/B
Am

D
G
C
G/B
Am
D
G
C
G/B
Am
D
G
C
Am
One day when the light

D
G
C
G/B
is glow - in', I'll be in my cas - tle gold - en.
Am
D
G
But un - til the gates are o - pen, I just wan - na feel
C
G/B
Am
D
this mo - ment. Whoa,
G
C
G/B
Am
I just wan - na feel this mo - ment. Whoa,

D
G
C
G/B
I just wan - na feel this mo - ment.
Am
D
G
C
G/B
Am
D
G
C
G/B
Am
Feel this mo - ment. Whoa,

Additional Lyrics

Rap 1: Reporting live from the tallest bulding in Tokyo.
Long way from them hard ways. Filled with so's and oh yeahs.
Dade County always. 305 all day.
Now, baby, we can parle. Or, baby, we can party.
She read books, especially about red rooms and tie ups.
I got her hooked 'cause she seen me in a suit with the red tie tied up.
Meet and greet, it's nice to meet ya, but time is money.
Only difference is, I own it. Now let's stop time and enjoy this moment.

Rap 2: I see the future but live for the moment. Makes sense, don't it, huh?
Now I make dollars, I mean billions. I'm a genius, I mean brilliance.
The streets is what schooled 'em and made 'em slicker than slick with the ruler.
I've lost a lot and learned a lot but I'm still undefeated like Shula.
I'm far from cheap. I break down companies with all my peeps.
Baby, we can travel the world and I can give you and all you can see.
Time is money. Only difference is, I own it.
Like a stop watch, let's stop time and enjoy this moment, dale.

FIRST TIME

Words and Music by KYRRE GØRVELL-DAHLL,
ALEXSEJ VLASENKO, HENRIK MEINKE,
JEREMY CHACON, JONAS KALISCH,
JENSON VAUGHAN, ELLIE GOULDING,
SARA HJELLSTROM and FANNY HULTMAN

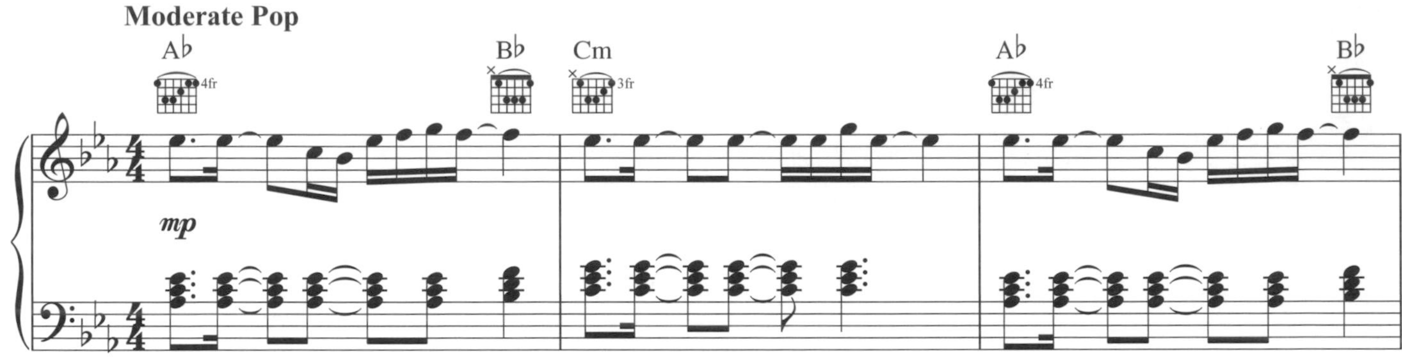

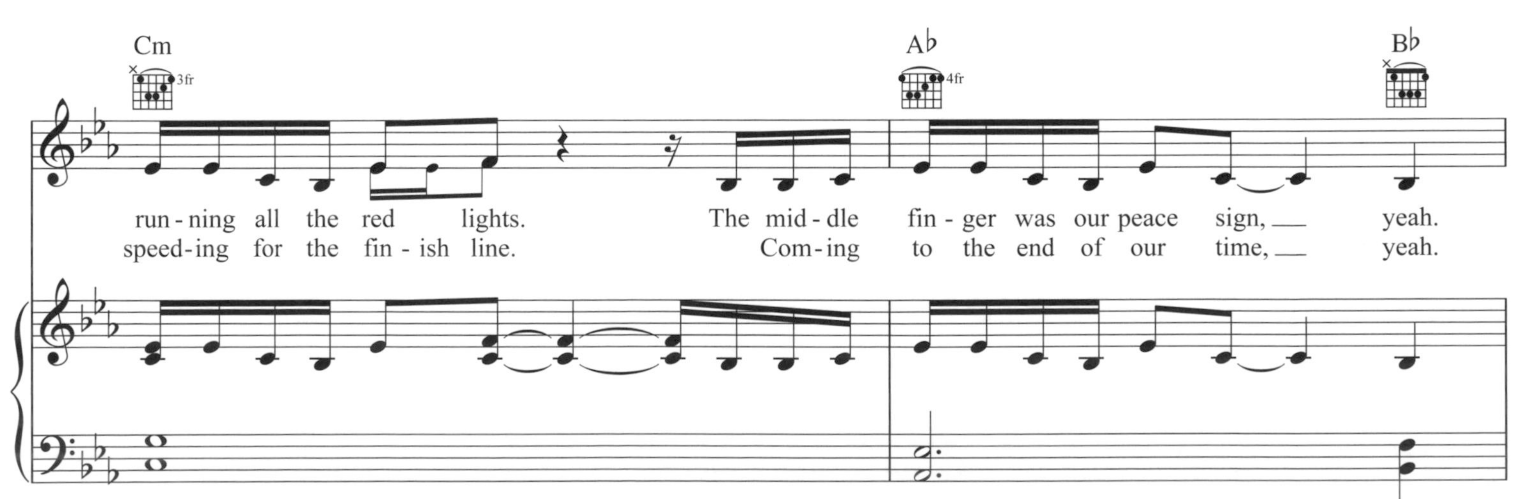

Cm
Ab
Bb
We were sip-ping on e-mo-tions, smok-ing and in-
Start-ed off as a wild-fire, burn-ing down the
Cm
Ab
Bb
hal-ing ev-'ry mo-ment. It was reck-less and we owned it, yeah, yeah.
bridg-es to our em-pire. Our love was some-thing they could ad-mire, yeah, yeah.
Cm
Eb
Ab
Bb
We were high and we were so-ber, we were un-der, we were
mf
Cm
Ab
Bb
Cm
N.C.
o-ver. We were young and now I'm old-er, but I'd do it all a-gain.
3fr
4fr

Ab
4fr
Bb
Cm
3fr
Get-ting drunk on a train track way back when we tried our first cig - a - rettes. Oh,
Ab
4fr
Bb
Cm
3fr
Eb
3fr
ten dol-lars was a fat stack. I'd do it all a - gain, oh.
Ab
4fr
Bb
Cm
3fr
Bought my jack - et and a snap - back, your dad's black Hon - da was our May - bach. Oh,
To Coda
Ab
4fr
Bb
Cm
3fr
Eb
3fr
three stacks on the play - back. I'd do it all a - gain, oh.

Ab Bb Cm Ab Bb

f

1 Cm Eb

2 Cm Eb

N.C. **D.S. al Coda**

We were

mp

CODA

Cm Eb Ab Bb Cm

it all a-gain, oh.

Ab Bb Cm Ab Bb

f

Cm
Eb
Ab
Bb
Stack, stack, stack, stack. All that I
think, think, think, think. All that I
try, try, try, try, ooh, oh,
try, try, try, try, ooh, all that.
Stack, stack, stack, stack. All that I
mp
think, think, think, think. All that I
try, try, try, try, oh,
try, try, try.

FIRESTONE

Words and Music by KYRRE GØRVELL-DAHLL,
MARTIJN KOIJNENBURG and CONRAD SEWELL

Em
Bm
A
G
I'm a flame, you're a fire. I'm the dark in need of light.
up, take me high - er. There's a world not far from here.
A
Bm
A
When we touch, you in - spire. Feel the
We can dance in de - sire or we can
G
1
Em
2
Em
change in me to - night. So take me
burn in love to - night. Our hearts a - live,
G
A
Bm
fire - stones, and when they strike we feel the love.

D
G
A
Sparks will fly,
they ig - nite our bones,
but when they strike
D
Bm
G
we light up the world.
Hearts a - live,
fire - stones,
A
Bm
D
and when they strike
we feel the love.
Sparks will fly,
G
A
D
To Coda
they ig - nite our bones,
but when they strike
we light up the world.

Bm
N.C.
We light up the world.
G
A
1
Bm
D
2
D
Bm
G
A
Bm
D
G
A

D
Bm
G
We light up the world,
A
Bm
D
oh,
world,
G
A
D
oh,
Bm
N.C.
Bm
fire - stone.
I'm from X,
you're from Y;

A
G
A
Bm
perfect strangers in the night.
Here we are, come together;
A
G
Em
to the world we'll testify.
N.C.
D.S. al Coda
Our hearts alive,
CODA
G
1
A
Bm
D

D
Bm
N.C.
G
We light up the world.
A
Bm
D
(Oh,
world.)
G
A
D
Bm
D
Bm
We light up the world.
Oh,
fire - stone.

FRIENDS

Words and Music by ANNE-MARIE NICHOLSON,
NATALIE MAREE DUNN, MARSHMELLO,
EDEN ANDERSON, SARAH BLANCHARD,
PABLO BOWMAN, RICHARD BOARDMAN
and JASMINE THOMPSON

Am C F E7sus E7
You're not my lov - er, more like a broth - er, I known you since we were, like, ten. Yeah!
two in the morn - ing, the rain is pour - ing. Have - n't we been here be - fore? Yeah!
Am C F E7sus E7
Don't mess it up, talk - ing that shit. On - ly gon - na push me a - way, that's it. When you
Don't mess it up, talk - ing that shit. On - ly gon - na push me a - way, that's it.
Am C F N.C.
say you love me, that make me cra - zy.
Have you got no shame? You look - ing in - sane.
Here we go a - gain. Don't go
Am C F E7sus E7 Am C
look at me with that look in your eye. You real - ly ain't go - ing a - way with - out a

F
E7sus
E7
Am
C
F
E7sus
E7
fight. You can't be rea-soned with; I'm done be - ing po - lite. I've told you
Am
C
F
E7sus
N.C.
one, two, three, four, five, six thou - sand times. Have - n't I made it
Am
C
F
ob - vi - ous? Have - n't I made it clear? Want me to spell it
Am
C
F
out for you? F - R - I - E - N - D - S. Have - n't I made it

Am
C
F
ob - vi - ous? Have - n't I made it clear? Want me to spell it
Am
C
F
out for you? F - R - I - E - N - D - S. F - R - I - E - N - D - S.
N.C. (F)
(G)
(Am)
(C)
F - R - I - E - N - D - S. That's how you **** - *** spell "friends."
(F)
(G)
(Dm)
(Em)
F - R - I - E - N - D - S. Get that shit in - side your head.

(F)
(G)
(Am)
(C)
No, no.
Yeah, uh, uh.
(Dm)
N.C.
F - R - I - E - N - D - S.
We're just friends. So don't go
Am
C
F
look at me with that look in your eye.
You real - ly
Am
C
F
ain't go - ing a - way with - out a fight.
You can't be

Am
C
F
rea - soned with, I'm done be - ing po - lite.
I've told you
Am
C
F
N.C.
one, two, three, four, five, six thou - sand times.
Have - n't I made it
Am
C
F
ob - vi - ous?
Have - n't I made it clear?
Want me to spell it
Am
C
F
out for you?
F - R - I - E - N - D - S.
Have - n't I made it

Am C F

ob - vi - ous? Have - n't I made it clear? Want me to spell it

Am C F

out for you? F - R - I - E N - D - S. F - R - I - E - N - D - S.

Am C F E7sus E7

Ooh, ooh, ooh, ooh. Ah,

Am C F E7sus E7

ah, ah.

HEY BROTHER

Words and Music by TIM BERGLING,
SALEM AL FAKIR, ASH POURNOURI,
VINCENT PONTARE and VERONICA MAGGIO

E♭
B♭
3fr
sis - ter, know the wa - ter's sweet, but
sis - ter, do you still be - lieve in
sis - ter, do you still be - lieve in
F
Gm
blood is thick - er.
love, I won - der.
love, I won - der.
F
B♭
E♭
F
Oh, if the sky comes fall - ing down for
B♭
E♭
you, there's noth - ing in this world I would-n't

Gm
3fr
do.
1
2, 3
N.C.
Ah.
Gm
3fr
E♭
3fr
B♭
What if I'm far from home?
Oh,
F/A
Gm
3fr
E♭
3fr
broth - er, I will hear you call.
What if I lose it
B♭
all?
Oh, sis - ter, I will help you out.

F
B♭
E♭
3fr
F
Oh, if the sky comes fall - ing down for
you, there's noth - ing in this world I would - n't
B♭
E♭
3fr
Gm
3fr
do.
Gm
3fr
E♭
3fr
F
Gm
3fr
B♭
F/A

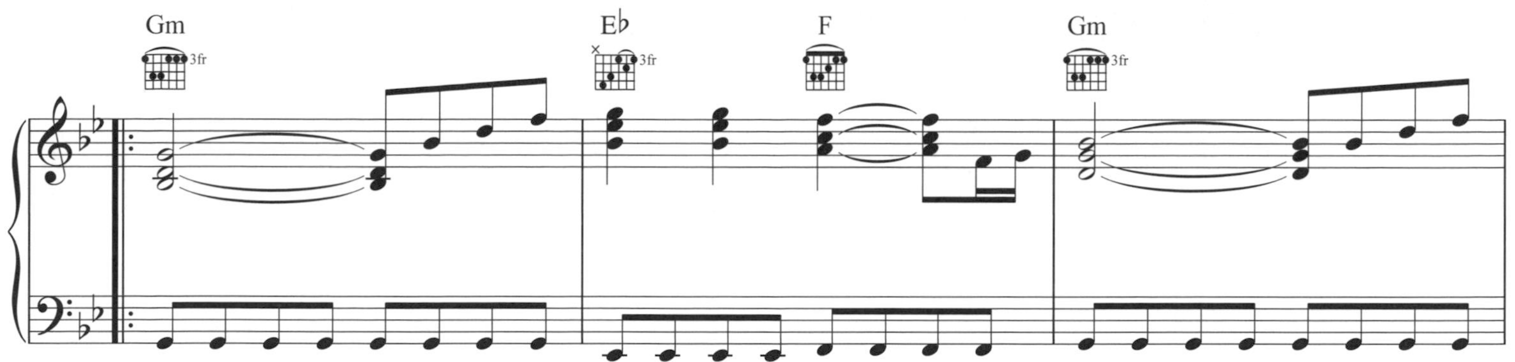
Gm
3fr
E♭
3fr
F
Gm
3fr

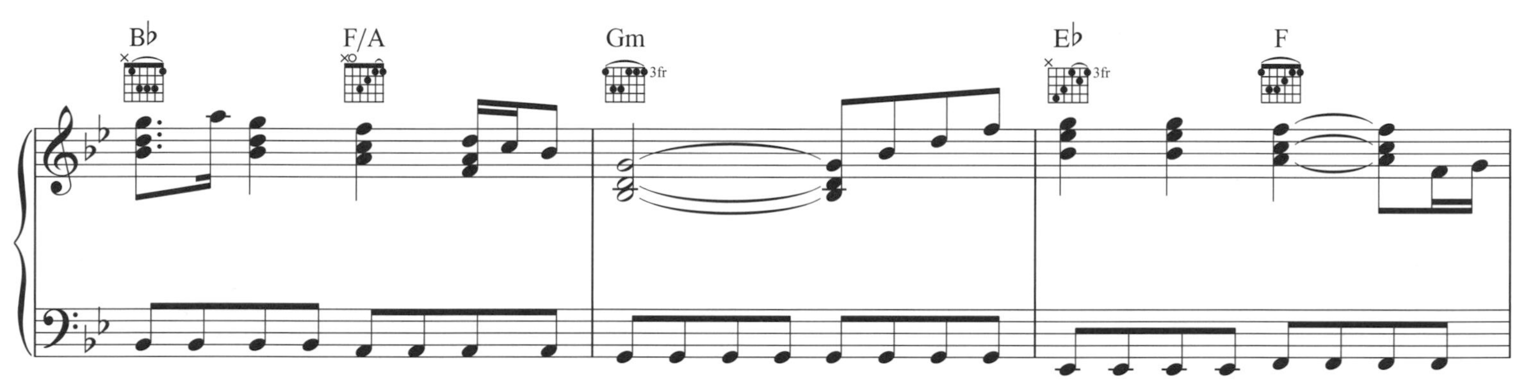
B♭
F/A
Gm
3fr
E♭
3fr
F

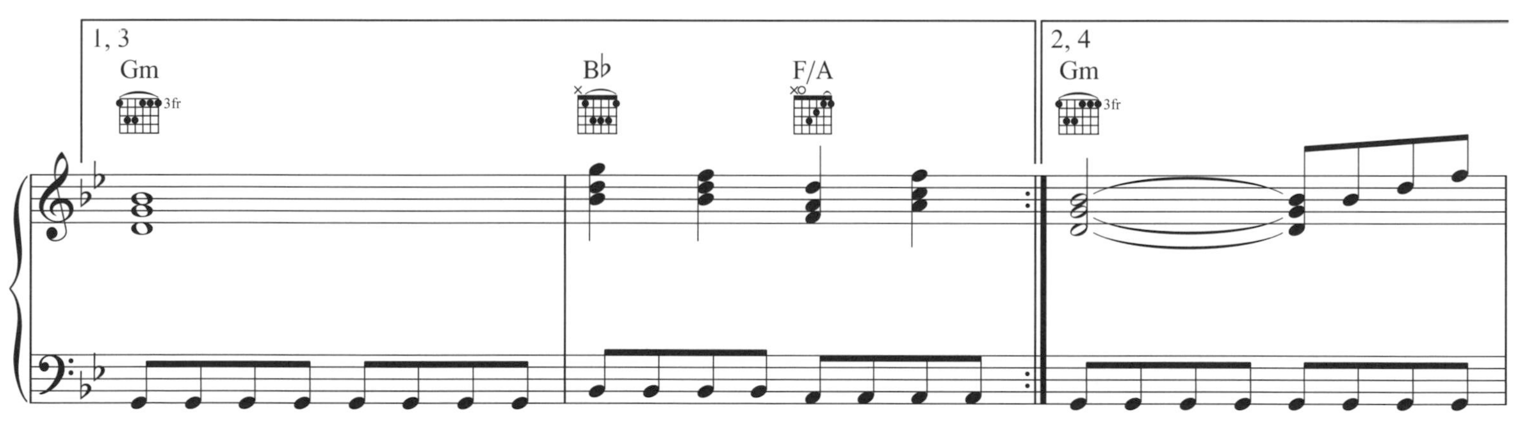
1, 3
Gm
3fr
B♭
F/A
2, 4
Gm
3fr

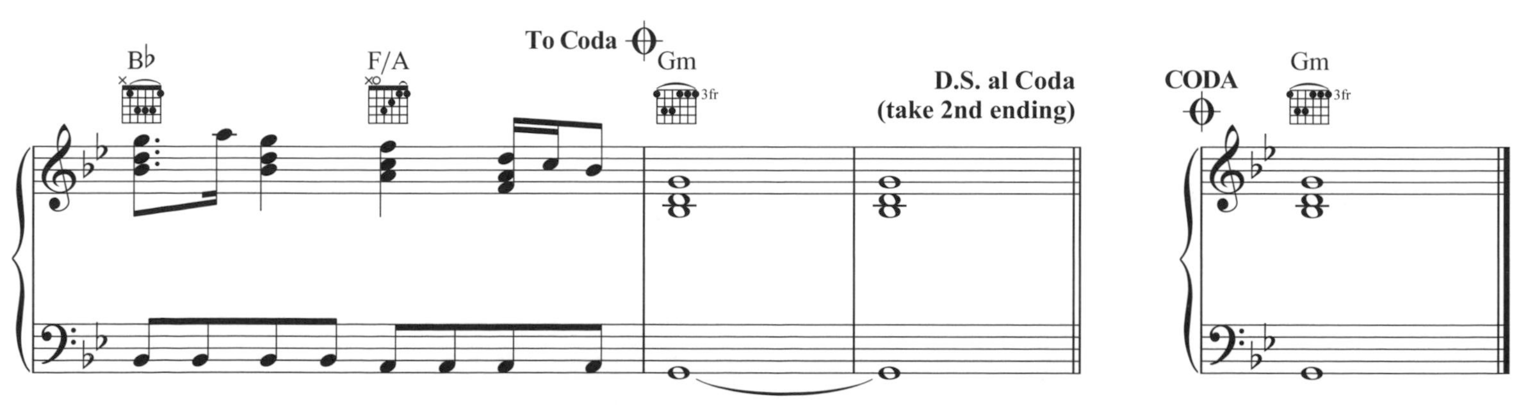
To Coda
B♭
F/A
Gm
3fr
D.S. al Coda
(take 2nd ending)
CODA
Gm
3fr

HOW DEEP IS YOUR LOVE

Words and Music by CALVIN HARRIS,
GAVIN KOOLMON, LUKE McDERMOTT,
NATHAN DUVALL and INA WROLDSEN

- y free - ly.
No in - hi - bi - tion,
no fear.
Em
Cmaj7
How deep is your love?
Is it like the o - cean?
What de - vo -
Em/A
Em
- tion are you?
How deep is your love?
Is it like nir - va -
Cmaj9
Em/A
- na?
Hit me hard - er a - gain.
How deep is your

Cmaj7
Em/A
love?
How deep is your love?
How deep is your love?
Cmaj7
Is it like the o - cean?
Pull me clos -
Em/A
N.C.
Em
- er a - gain.
How deep is your love?
Ah, ah, ooh.
Cmaj7
Em/A
Ah, ah, ooh.
Ah, ah, ooh.
How deep is your

Em
Cmaj9
Em/A
To Coda
love? Ah, ah, ooh. Ah, ah, ooh. Ah, ah, ooh.
N.C.
O-pen up my eyes and tell me who I am.
Am
C
Let me in on all your se-crets.
Am
D.S. al Coda
No in-hi-bi-tion, no sin. How deep is your
3

CODA
Em
Cmaj7
How deep is your love?
(So, tell me: how deep is your love?
Em/A
Can it go deep - er?
So, tell me: how deep is your love?
Em
Cmaj9
Can it go deep?
So, tell me: how deep is your love?
Em/A
Can it go deep - er?
So tell me, how deep is your love?

Cmaj7
How deep is your love?
Can it go deep?
So, tell me: how deep is your love?
Em/A
Can it go deep - er?
So, tell me: how deep is your love?
Cmaj7
How deep is your love?
Can it go deep?
So, tell me: how deep is your love?
Em/A
Pull me clos - er a - gain.
Can it go deep - er?
So, tell me: how deep is your love?)

N.C.
Em
How deep is your love? Ah, ah, ooh.
3
Cmaj7
Em/A
Ah, ah, ooh. Ah, ah, ooh.
Em
How deep is your love? Ah, ah, ooh.
Cmaj9
Em/A
Ah, ah, ooh. Ah, ah, ooh. How deep is your

Em
Cmaj7
love? (So, tell me: how deep is your love? Can it go deep - er?
Em/A
How deep is your
So, tell me: how deep is your love? Can it go deep?
Em
Cmaj9
love? So, tell me: how deep is your love? Can it go deep - er?
Em/A
So, tell me: how deep is your love? Can it go deep?)

LEAN ON

Words and Music by KAREN MARIE ØRSTED,
THOMAS PENTZ, WILLIAM GRIGAHCINE,
STEVE GUESS and PHILIP MECKSEPER

Gm
B♭
E♭maj7
F
3fr
we were bold _ and young.
long - ing for you to come home?
All a - round _ the wind blows, _
All a - round _ the wind blows, _
𝄋
we would on - ly hold _ on to let go.
we would on - ly hold _ on to let go.
Blow a kiss, fi - re a gun, _
_ we all need some - one to lean on.
Blow a kiss, fi - re a gun,
all we need is some-bod - y to lean on.
Blow a kiss, fi - re a gun, _

Gm
3fr
B♭
E♭maj7
3fr
F
To Coda
we all need some - one to lean on. Blow a kiss, fi - re a gun,
N.C.
E♭maj7
F
all we need is some - bod - y to lean on. Hey ho, hey ho.
Gm
B♭
E♭maj7
F
Hey ho, hey ho. Hey ho, hey ho.
1
Gm
E♭maj7
F
Hey ho, hey ho. Hey ho, hey ho.

Gm
3fr
B♭
E♭maj7
3fr
F
Hey ho, hey ho. Hey ho, hey ho.
Gm
3fr
Hey ho, hey ho.
2
Gm
3fr
All we need is some-bod - y to lean on.
E♭maj7
3fr
F
Gm
3fr
B♭
Hey ho, hey ho. Hey ho, hey ho.
E♭maj7
3fr
F
Gm
3fr
Hey ho, hey ho. All we need is some-bod - y to lean on,

N.C.
Ebmaj7
F
lean on, lean on, lean on, lean on, lean on, hey!
Gm
Bb
Ebmaj7
F
Gm
Bb
Ebmaj7
F
Gm
Bb
Ebmaj7
F
Gm
D.S. al Coda
CODA
Gm
All we need is some - bod - y to lean on.

HEY MAMA

Words and Music by DAVID GUETTA,
ONIKA MARAJ, ESTER DEAN,
NICK VAN DE WALL, BEBE REXHA,
GIORGIO TUINFORT, SEAN DOUGLAS,
ALAN LOMAX and JOHN LOMAX

Yes, I be your girl, for - ev - er your la - dy. You ain't ev - er got - ta wor - ry. I'm down for you, ba - by.
Yes, you be the boss and, yes, I'll be re - spect - ing. What - ev - er that you tell me 'cause it's game you be spit - ting.
E5
Best be - lieve that, when you need that, I'll pro - vide that. You will al - ways have it.
I'll be on deck, keep it in check. When you need that, I'm a let you have it.
Em
C
Am
D
Beat - ing my drum like dum - di - di - day, I like the dirt - y rhy - thm you play.

Em
C
Am
D
I wan - na hear you call - in' my name like hey ma - ma, ma - ma. Hey ma - ma, ma.
Bang - in' the drum like dum - di - di - day, I know you want it in the worst way.
I wan - na hear you call - in' my name like hey ma - ma, ma - ma. Hey ma - ma, ma.
To Coda
Be my wom - an, girl, and I'll be your man. Be my wom - an, girl, and I'll

N.C.
be your man.
Rap: (See additional lyrics)
So, ba - by, when you need that, give me the
word. I'm no good, I'll be bad for my babe. So I
Em
C
make sure that he's get - tin' his share,

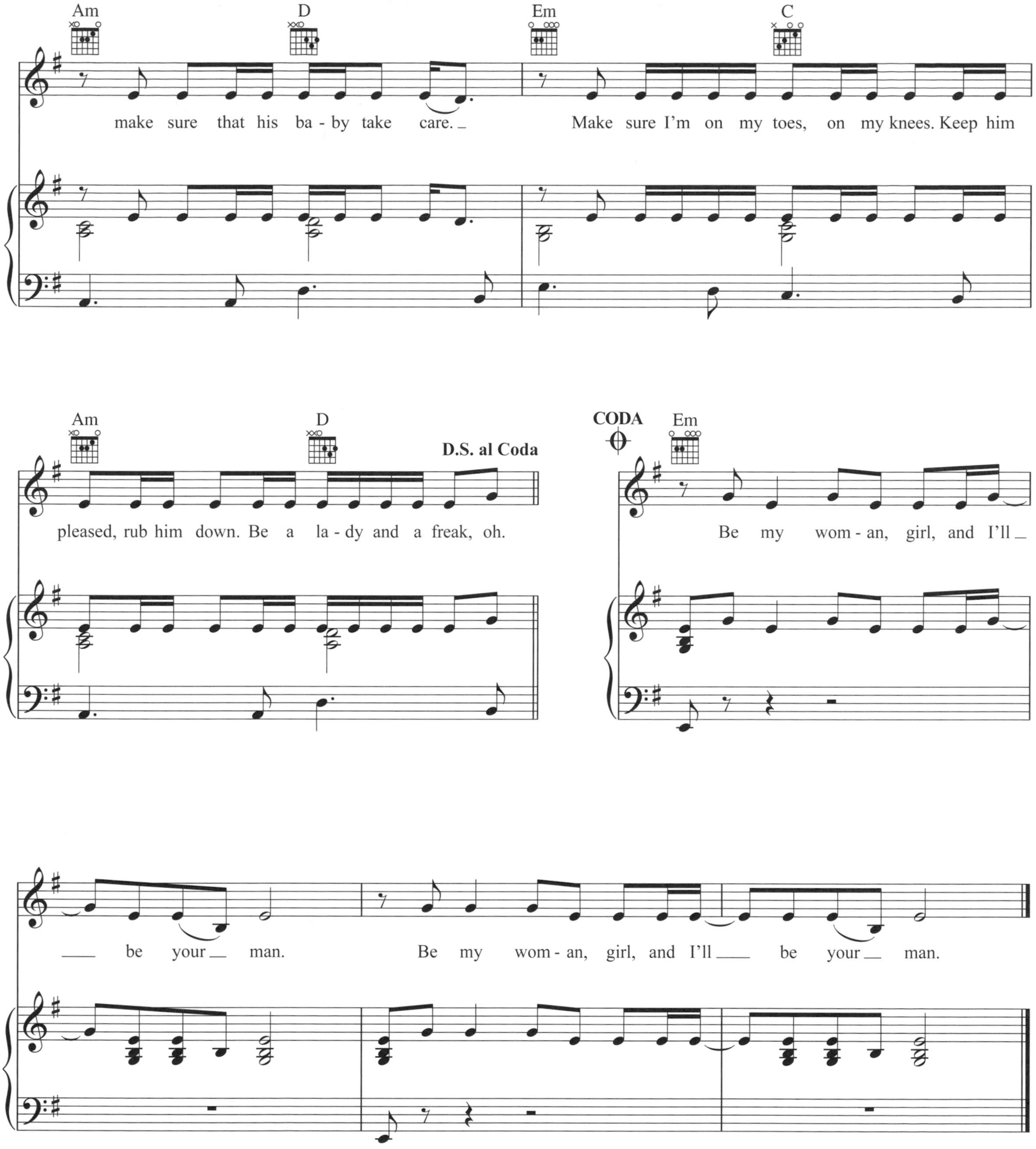

Am D Em C

make sure that his ba - by take care. _ Make sure I'm on my toes, on my knees. Keep him

Am D **D.S. al Coda** **CODA** Em

pleased, rub him down. Be a la - dy and a freak, oh. Be my wom - an, girl, and I'll _

Additional Lyrics

Rap: Whole crew got the juice. Your dick came the truth.
My screams is the proof. Them other dudes get the deuce.
When I speed in the coupe leavin' this interview,
It ain't nothin' new. I been f***in' with you.
None of them bitches ain't takin' you, just tell 'em to make a U.
That's how it be. I come first like debut.

LET ME GO

Words and Music by ALI TAMPOSI,
ANDREW WOTMAN, JAMIE LIDDERDALE,
ALESSANDRO LINBALD and BRIAN LEE

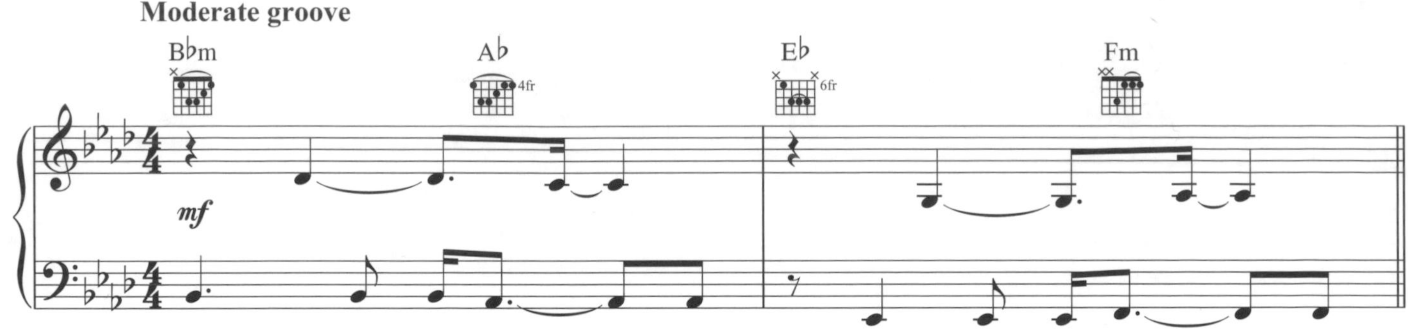

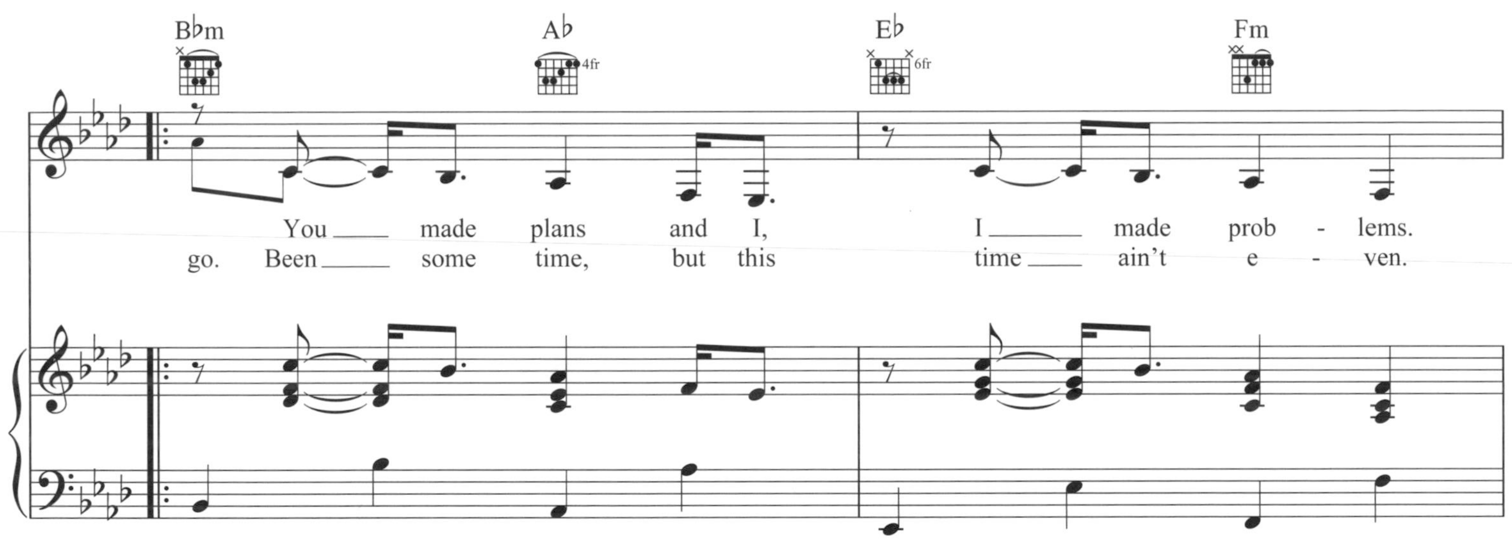

D♭
A♭
E♭
Fm
good on pa - per, pic - ture per - fect.
B♭m
A♭
E♭
Fm
Chased the high too far, too fast. Pick - et white fence but we paint it black. (Ooh,)
B♭m
A♭
E♭
Fm
and I wish you would
and I wish that you would
hurt me hard - er than I hurt you. (Ooh,)
B♭m
A♭
E♭
N.C.
and I wish you would - n't wait for me, but you al - ways do.

D♭
A♭
E♭
Fm
4fr
6fr
I've been hop - in' some - bod - y loves you in the ways I could - n't.
B♭m
Some - bod - y's tak - in' care of all of the mess I made,
some - one you don't have to change. I've been hop - in'
some - one will love you. Let me go.

D♭
A♭
E♭
Fm
B♭m
Some - one will love you; let me go.
I've been hop - in' some - one will love you. Let me
go.
Some - one will love you; let me go.
Some-one will love you; let me go.
Some - one will love you; let me
4fr
6fr
4fr

D♭
A♭
E♭
Fm
4fr
6fr
go.
Some - one will love you; let me go.
I've been hop - in'
some - bod - y loves you in the ways I could - n't.
Some - bod - y's tak - in' care of
B♭m
all of the mess I made,
some - one you don't have to change.
I've been hop - in'
some - one will love you. Let me go.
N.C.

I LOVE IT

Words and Music by CHARLOTTE AITCHISON,
LINUS EKLOW and PATRIK BERGER

D♭5
4fr
N.C.
A♭5
4fr
I crashed my car in - to the bridge. I don't care, I love it.
D♭5
4fr
I don't care.
A♭5
4fr
I got this feel - in' on the sum - mer day when you were gone.
D♭5
4fr
I crashed my car in - to the bridge. I watched, I let it burn.

A♭5
4fr
I threw your sh** in - to a bag and pushed it down the stairs.
D♭5
4fr
I crashed my car in - to the bridge. I don't
A♭5
4fr
care, I love it. I don't
D♭5
4fr
care. You're on a

B♭5
C♭5
dif - f'rent road, I'm in the Milk - y Way. You want me
D♭5
4fr
down on Earth, but I am up in space. You're so damn
B♭5
C♭5
hard to please. We got - ta kill this switch. You're from the
D♭5
4fr
To Coda
N.C.
sev - en - ties, but I'm a nine - ties bitch. I love it.

A♭5
4fr
D♭5
4fr
A♭5
4fr
I love it.
D♭5
4fr
A♭5
4fr
I got this feel - in' on the
sum-mer day when you were gone.
D♭5
4fr
I crashed my car in - to the bridge.

Ab5
4fr
I watched, I let it burn.
I threw your sh** in - to a bag
Db5
4fr
and pushed it down the stairs.
I crashed my car in - to the bridge.
Ab5
4fr
I don't care,
I love it.
I don't
Db5
4fr
care,
I love it,
I love it.
I don't
Ab5
4fr
care,
I love it.

Db5
4fr
D.S. al Coda
I don't care. _
You're on a
CODA
N.C.
Ab5
4fr
nine - ties _ bitch. I don't care, _ I love it. I don't
Db5
4fr
Ab5
4fr
care, _ I love it, I love it. I don't care, _
Db5
4fr
I love it.

LET ME LOVE YOU

Words and Music by JUSTIN BIEBER,
CARL ROSEN, WILLIAM GRIGAHCINE,
EDWIN PEREZ, TEDDY MENDEZ,
ANDREW WOTMAN, ALEXANDRA TAMPOSI,
LOUIS BELL, LUMIDEE CEDEÑO,
BRIAN LEE and STEVEN MARSDEN

Moderate Pop

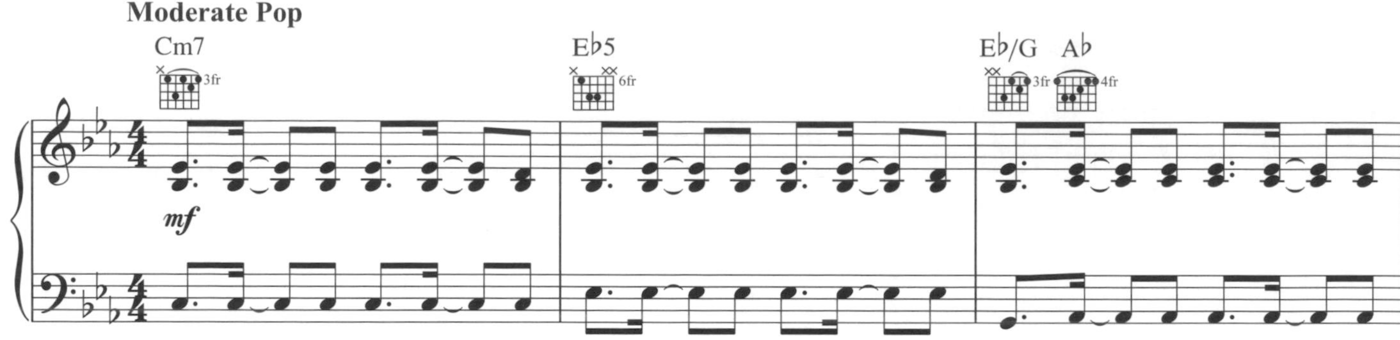

Cm7
Eb5
Eb/G
Ab
smoke and mir - rors keep us wait - ing on a mir - a - cle, on a
is a rude a - wak - en - ing to know we're good e - nough, oh, we're
Eb/G
Ab
Cm7
mir - a - cle.
good e - nough.
Say, go through the dark - est of days, heav - en's a heart - break a - way.
Bb
Fm7
Ab
Nev - er let you go, nev - er let me down.
Oh, it's been a hell of a ride,
Cm9
Bb
driv - ing the edge of a knife. Nev - er let you go, nev - er let me down.

Fm7
Cm7
Don't you give up, na, na, na. I won't give up,
Ebmaj7
Eb/G Ab
na, na, na. Let me love you, let me love you.
Don't you give up,
Cm7
Ebmaj7
na, na, na. I won't give up, na, na, na. Let me
Eb/G Ab
N.C.
Cm7
love you, let me love you.

E♭
3fr
E♭/G
3fr
A♭
4fr
E♭/G
3fr
A♭
4fr

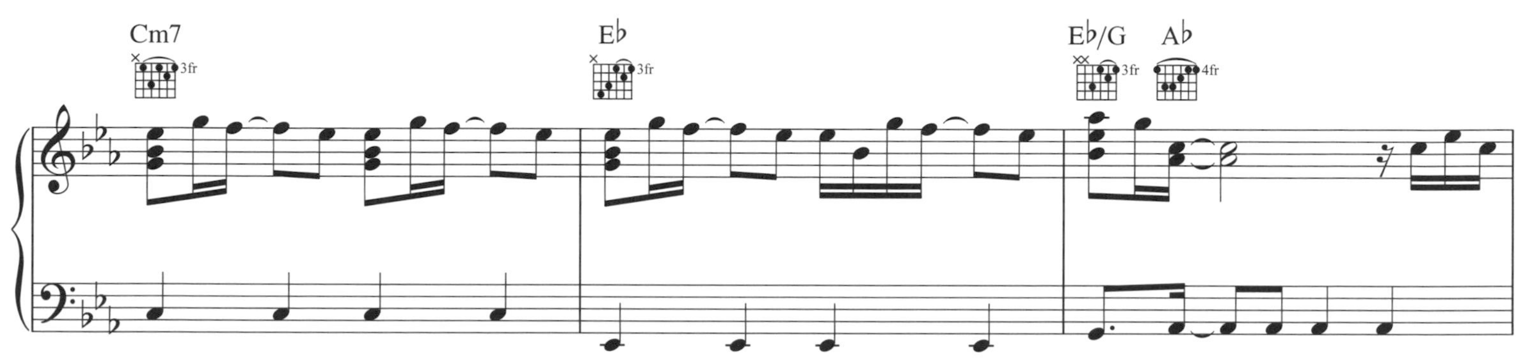

Cm7
3fr
E♭
3fr
E♭/G
3fr
A♭
4fr

1
E♭/G
3fr
A♭
4fr
2
E♭/G
3fr
A♭
4fr
Cm7
3fr
Don't fall a - sleep

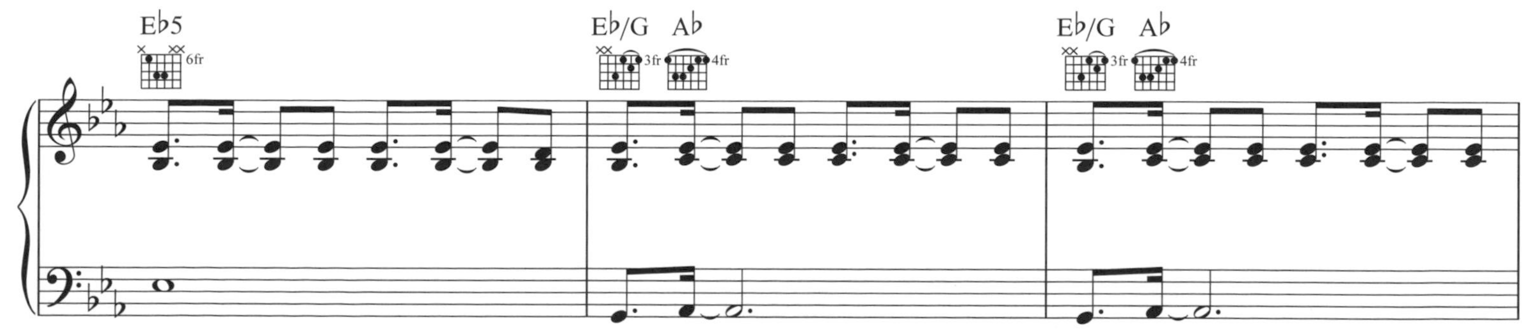

E♭5
6fr
E♭/G
3fr
A♭
4fr
E♭/G
3fr
A♭
4fr

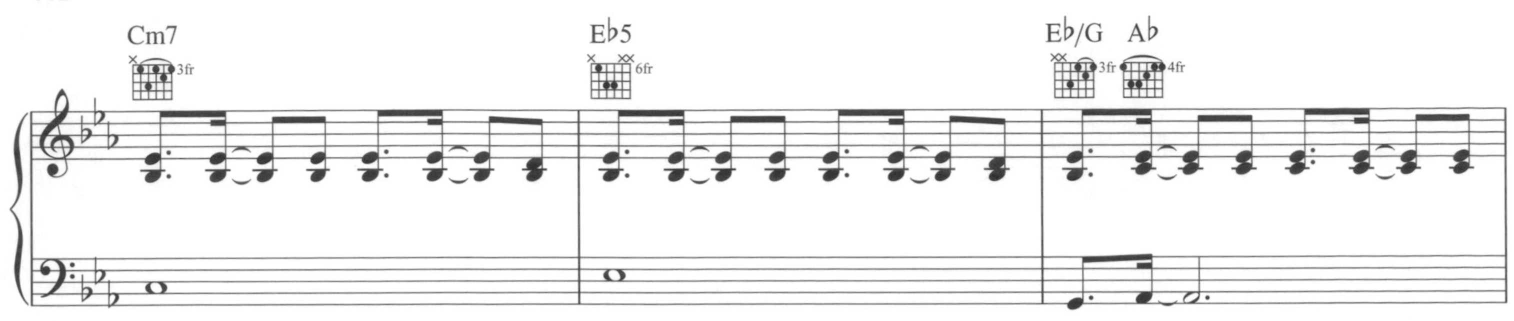
Cm7
E♭5
E♭/G
A♭
3fr
6fr
4fr

E♭/G
A♭
Cm7
E♭maj7
Don't you give up, na, na, na. I won't give up, na, na, na. Let me

E♭/G
A♭
E♭/G
A♭
Cm7
love you, let me love you. Don't you give up, na, na, na. I won't give up,

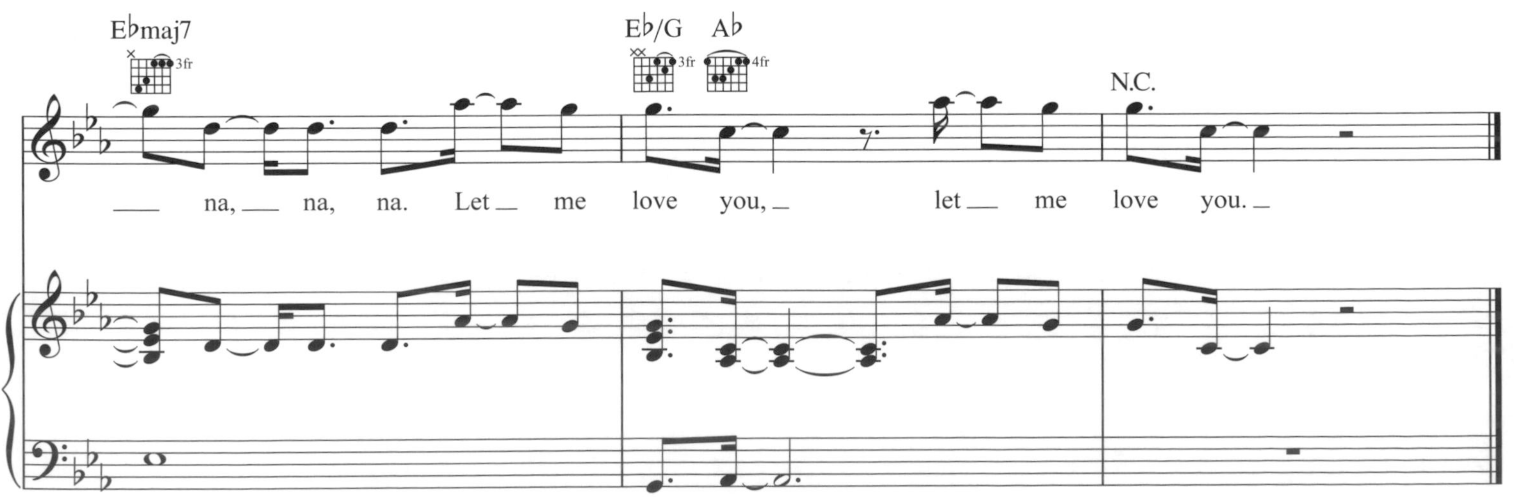
E♭maj7
E♭/G
A♭
N.C.
na, na, na. Let me love you, let me love you.

IT AIN'T ME

Words and Music by ALI TAMPOSI,
SELENA GOMEZ, ANDREW WOTMAN,
KYRRE GØRVELL-DAHLL and BRIAN LEE

F
C
F
C
see - ing eye to eye. You were stay - ing out all night, and I
oids and the mem - o - ries, but you know I'm gon - na leave be - hind the worst
Play 1st time only
G
Am
C
had e - nough. No, I don't wan - na know where you been
F
C
F
C
or where you're go - ing. But I know I won't be home, and you'll be on
G
F
C
your own.
of us.
Who's gon - na walk you through the dark side of the morn-

G
F
C
- ing? Who's gon - na rock you when the sun won't let you sleep?
G
F
C
Who's wak - ing up to drive you home when you're drunk
G
G♯dim
Am
F
C
To Coda
and all a - lone? Who's gon - na walk you through the dark side of the morn-
G
Am
C
G
F
- ing? It ain't me.

Am C G F C

(It ain't me.)

Am G F C G N.C.

(It ain't

Am C G F Am C

me.)

G F C Am G

(It ain't me.)

F C G Am C
D.S. al Coda
It ain't me.
CODA
G F C G
- ing? It ain't me, (no, no.) It ain't
F C G F C
me, (no, no.) It ain't me, (no, no.)
G G♯dim Am F C
3fr
Who's gon - na walk you through the dark side of the morn -

G
Am
C
G
F
- ing? It ain't me.
Am
C
G
(It ain't
F
C
Am
G
me.)
F
C
G
N.C.

Am
C
G
F
me.)
Am
C
G
F
C
(It ain't
me.)
Am
G
1
F
C
G
(It ain't
2
F
C
G
N.C.
It ain't
me.

THE MIDDLE

Words and Music by SARAH AARONS,
MARCUS LOMAX, JORDAN JOHNSON,
ANTON ZASLAVSKI, KYLE TREWARTHA,
MICHAEL TREWARTHA and STEFAN JOHNSON

Csus2
G
D
Csus2
3fr
3fr
closer. Why don't you pull me close? Why don't you come on over? I can't just let you
go. Oh, baby, why don't you just meet me in the
G
D
Cmaj7
G
D
Am7
Cmaj7
Em7
D
Am7
Cmaj7
middle? I'm losing my mind just a little. So,
Em7
D
Am7
Cmaj7
G
D
why don't you just meet me in the middle, in the middle?

Cmaj7
G
D
C
Ba - by,
why don't you just meet me in the
mid - dle?
I'm
Em7
D
C
G
D
C
los - ing
my mind
just
a
lit - tle.
So,
why don't you
just meet me
in
the
To Coda
Em7
D
C
mid - dle,
in
the
mid - dle?
Take
a
step
G
D
C
back
for
a
min
-
ute,
in - to
the
kitch
-
en.
Floors
are
wet
and

G
D
C
taps are still run - ning, dish - es are bro - ken. How did we get in - to this
G
D
C
Em
D
C
mess, got so ag-gres - sive? I know we meant all good in - ten - tions, so pull me
G
D
C
clos - er. Why don't you pull me close? Why don't you come on o - ver? I can't just let you
G
D
D.S. al Coda
go. Oh.
CODA
Am7
G/B
C
Look-ing at you, I can't lie, just pour-ing out ad -

G D Am7 G/B
mis - sion, re - gard - less of my ob - jec - tion. Oh, oh, and it's not a - bout my
C Em D
pride. I need you on my skin, just come o - ver, pull me in, just... Oh,
C G D C
ba - by, why don't you just meet me in the mid - dle? I'm
G D C G D C
los - ing my mind just a lit - tle. So, why don't you just meet me in the

G
D
C
(with vocal ad lib.)
mid - dle, in the mid - dle? No, no. Ba - by,
G
D
C
Em7
D
C
why don't you just meet me in the mid - dle? I'm los - ing my mind just a
G
D
C
1
lit - tle. So, why don't you just meet me in the mid - dle, in the
Em7
D
2
Em7
D
mid - dle? mid - dle, mid - dle, in the mid - dle, mid - dle?

ONE KISS

Words and Music by JESSICA REYES,
CALVIN HARRIS and DUA LIPA

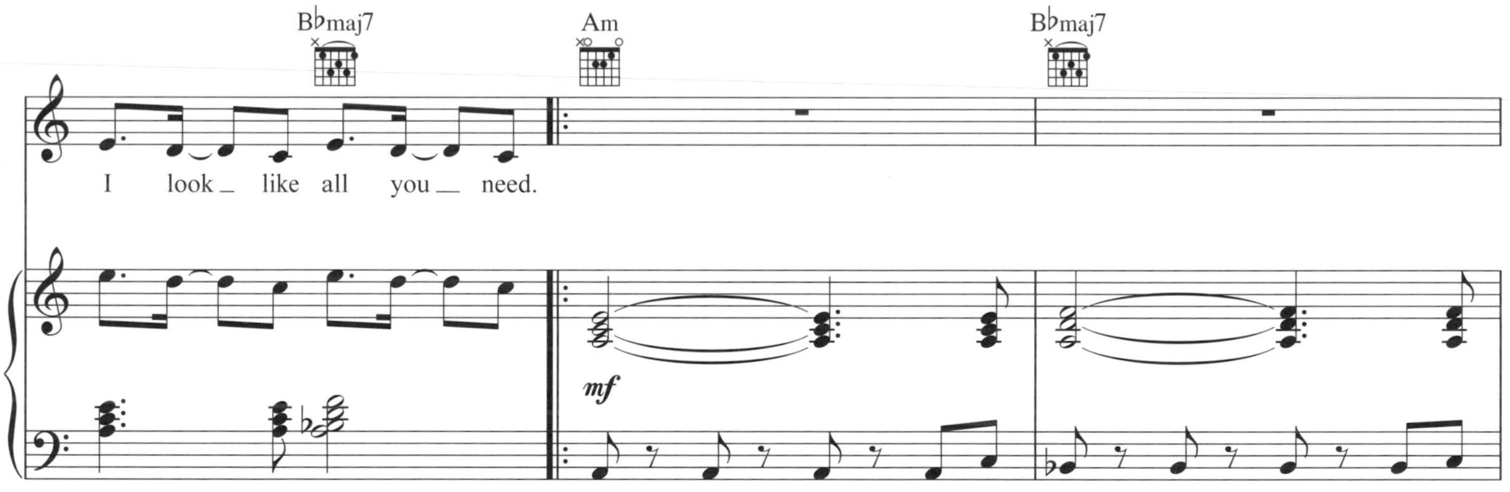

Am
Bbmaj7
take the night, I love real eas - y
and I
Fmaj7
Gm9
3fr
know that you'll still wan - na see me.
On the
Am
Bbmaj7
Sun - day morn - ing, mu - sic real loud,
let me
Fmaj7
Gm9
3fr
love you while the moon is still out.

Am
Bbmaj7
Some - thing in you lit up

Fmaj7
Gm9
3fr
Am
heav - en in me. The feel - ing won't let me sleep,

Bbmaj7
Fmaj7
Gm9
3fr
'cause I'm lost in the way you move, the way you feel.

Fmaj7
Gm9
3fr
Am
pos - si-bil-i-ties, I look like all you need. One kiss is all it takes,
Bb maj7
Fmaj7
Gm9
3fr
To Coda
fall - in' in love with me, pos - si-bil-i-ties, I look like all you need.
Am
Bb maj7
Fmaj7
Gm9
3fr
G/A
Bb maj7
I just wan - na feel your skin on mine,

Fmaj7
Gm9
3fr
G/A
feel your eyes do the ex - plor - ing, pas -
B♭maj7
Fmaj7
- sion in the mes - sage when you smile, take my time.
F/G
Am
B♭maj7
Some - thing in you lit up
Fmaj7
Gm9
3fr
Am
heav - en in me. The feel - ing won't let me sleep,

D.S. al Coda
B♭maj7
Fmaj7
Gm9
3fr
'cause I'm lost in the way you move, the way you feel.
CODA
Am
B♭maj7
Fmaj7
Gm9
3fr
Fmaj7
Gsus
See won - der -
mp
Am7
B♭maj7
Fmaj7
land in your eyes.

Gsus Am7 B♭maj7

Might need your com - pa - ny to - night.

Fmaj7 F/G G/A

Some - thing in you lit up heav - en in me.

B♭maj7 Fmaj7 F/G

The feel - ing won't let me sleep, 'cause I'm

B♭maj7
Fmaj7
Gm9
3fr
fall - in' in love with me, pos - si - bil - i - ties, I look like all you need.
Am
B♭maj7
Fmaj7
One kiss is all it takes, fall - in' in love with me, pos - si - bil - i - ties,
Gm9
3fr
Am
B♭maj7
I look like all you need.
Fmaj7
1
Gm9
3fr
2
Gm9
3fr

PERFECT STRANGERS

Words and Music by JOHN COOPER, ALEX SMITH and JONAS BLUE

* Recorded a half step lower.

D5
A5
G5
wast-ing your time, I'm not play-ing no games,
May-be we're help-ing each oth-er es-cape,
I see you.
I'm with you.
B5
Who knows the se-cret to-mor-row will hold?
We don't real-ly need to know
'cause you're here with me now, I don't want you to go.
5fr
3fr
7fr

D5
A5
5fr
G5
3fr
You're here with me now, I don't want you to go.
G
A
Bm
May - be we're per - fect stran - gers, may - be it's not for - ev - er,
D5
A
G
may - be the light will change us, may - be we'll stay to - geth - er.
A
Bm
May - be we'll walk a - way, may - be we'll re - al - ize

D5
A
G
we're on - ly hu - man, may - be we don't need no rea - son.
A
Bm
May - be we're per - fect stran - gers, may - be it's not for - ev - er,
D5
A
G
may - be the light will change us, may - be we'll stay to - geth - er.
A
Bm
May - be we'll walk a - way, may - be we'll re - al - ize

D5
A
N.C.
we're on - ly hu - man, may - be we don't need no rea - son
G5
A5
3fr
5fr
B5
7fr
D5
A5
G5
why. Come on, come on, come on now.
May - be we don't need no rea - son why. Come
on, come on, come on now.

A5
5fr
B5
7fr
Come on, come on, come on now.
D5
A5
5fr
G5
3fr
May - be we don't need no rea - son
G5
3fr
A5
5fr
B5
7fr
why.
Come on, come on, come on now.
D5
A5
5fr
G5
3fr
N.C.

RATHER BE

Words and Music by GRACE CHATTO,
JACK PATTERSON, NICOLE MARSHALL
and JAMES NAPIER

* Recorded a half step lower.

Am G6 F C Fmaj7 Dm
long as you are with me, there's no place I'd rath - er be.
make it ev - er - last - ing, so noth - ing's in - com - plete.
F G6 Am G6 F C
I would wait for - ev - er, ex -
It's eas - y be - ing with you: sa -
Am G6 F C Am G6
ult - ed in the scene. As long as I am with
cred sim - plic - i - ty. As long as we're to - geth -
F C Fmaj7 Dm
you, my heart con - tin - ues to beat.
- er, there's no place I'd rath - er be.

F
G6
Am
Fmaj7
With ev - 'ry step we take,
Em7
Am11
3fr
Ky - o - to to the Bay, stroll - ing so cas - ual - ly,
Fmaj7
Em7
we're dif - f'rent and the same. Get you an - oth - er name,
Am11
3fr
Am
G
Am
Em7
switch up the bat - ter - ies. If you gave me a chance,

Fmaj9
C
G/B
Am
Em7
I would take it. It's a shot in the dark,
Fmaj9
C
G/B
Am
G
but I'll make it. Know with all of your heart,
Fmaj9
C
Dm7
you can't shake me. When I am with you, there's
Fmaj7
G♯dim
3fr
Am7
Em7
no place I'd rath - er be. No, no, no, no, no,

Fmaj7
G♯dim
3fr
Am7
Em7
Fmaj7
no place I'd rath - er be.
No, no, no, no, no,
G♯dim
3fr
Am7
Em7
Fmaj7
no place I'd rath - er be.
No, no, no, no, no,
To Coda
1
G6
Dm7
Fmaj7
no place I'd rath - er be.
We
2
N.C.
When I am with you, there's no place I'd rath - er be.

Am
G6
F
C/E
Am
G6
F
C/E
Am
G6
F
C/E
D.S. al Coda
Fmaj7
Dm
C/E
G
Yeah, y - yeah, y - yeah, y - yeah, y - yeah, __ yeah, yeah.
CODA
Dm7
Fmaj7
When I __ am with you, _ there's no place _ I'd rath - er be. ________

SCARED TO BE LONELY

Words and Music by GEORGIA OVERTON,
GIORGIO TUINFORT, NATE CAMPANY,
MARTIJN GARRITSEN and KYLE SHEARER

A
C♯m
4fr
B
and slam - ming doors, mag - ni - fy - ing all our flaws.
and slam - ming doors, mag - ni - fy - ing all our flaws.
Emaj7/G♯
A
C♯m
4fr
And I won - der why, won - der what for, why we keep
And I won - der why, won - der what for. It's like we keep
B
Emaj7/G♯
A
com - ing back for more.
com - ing back for more.
Is it
E
B
C♯m
4fr
just our bod - ies? Are we both los - ing our minds?

A
E
B
Is the on - ly rea - son you're hold - ing me to - night 'cause we're scared
C#m
4fr
A
E
to be lone - ly? Do we need some - bod - y
B
C#m
4fr
A
just to feel like we're al - right? Is the on - ly
E
B
N.C.
rea - son you're hold - ing me to - night 'cause we're scared to be lone - ly?

1
A
E
B
C♯m
4fr
A
E
B
G♯m7
4fr
C♯m
4fr
Too much _ time _
2
A
E
B
C♯m
4fr
Scared _ to be lone - ly. _
A
E
B
G♯m7
4fr
C♯m
4fr
Ooh. _
E -

A
C#m
4fr
B
- ven when we know it's wrong, been some-bod-y bet - ter for us all a -
Emaj7/G#
A
C#m
4fr
long. Tell me, how can we keep hold - ing on, hold - ing on
B
Emaj7/G#
A
to-night 'cause we're scared to be lone - ly? E - ven when we know it's
C#m
4fr
B
Emaj7/G#
wrong, been some-bod-y bet - ter for us all a - long. Tell me, how

A
C♯m
4fr
B
can we keep hold - ing on, hold - ing on tonight 'cause we're scared
Emaj7/G♯
A
E
to be lone - ly? Is it just our bod - ies?
B
C♯m
4fr
A
Are we both los - ing our minds? Is the on - ly
E
B
N.C.
rea - son you're hold - ing me to - night 'cause we're scared to be lone - ly?

A
E
B
C#m
4fr
A
E
B
G#m7
4fr
C#m
4fr
Scared _ to be lone - ly. ___
A
E
B
C#m
4fr
Ooh. ___
Scared _ to be lone - ly. ___
A
E
B
G#m7
4fr
C#m
4fr
Ooh, ___
eh, eh, scared _ to be lone - ly.

NEVER FORGET YOU

Words and Music by ZARA LARSSON,
UZOECHI EMENIKE and ARRON DAVEY

Em
Bm
G
time has-n't changed a thing.
It's ver-y deep in-side me, but I
Em
feel there's some-thing you should know.
Mm.
I will
Bm
G
A
nev-er for-get you,
and you'll al-ways be by my side.
From the
Bm
G
day that I met you,
I knew that I would love you till the day I

Em
Bm
G
die. And I will nev - er want much more, and in my heart
A
Bm
G
I will al - ways be sure that I will nev - er for - get you,
To Coda
N.C.
and you'll al - ways be by my side till the day I die.
Bm
G
(Oh, oh, oh,

A
Bm
G
oh.) Till the day I die. (Oh, oh,
Em
Bm
oh, oh.) (Yeah, yeah, yeah,
G
A
yeah, yeah, yeah, yeah, yeah, yeah, yeah.) Till the day I die.
Bm
G
(Yeah, yeah, yeah, yeah, yeah, yeah, yeah, yeah, yeah,

Em
N.C.
G
yeah.)
Fun-ny how we both end up here, but ev-'ry-thing seems so right.
Em
Bm
I won-der what would hap-pen if we
G
Em
went back and put up a fight.
'Cause once up-on a
Bm
G
time, you were my ev-'ry-thing.
It's clear to see that time has-n't changed a

Em
Bm
thing. So, what in this world do you think could
G
Em
D.S. al Coda
ev - er take you off my mind? I will
CODA
Em
G
Do - in' it, lov - in' it, ev - 'ry - thing that we do. And
Feel - in' it, lov - in' it, ev - 'ry - thing that we do. And
Bm
D
all a - long, I knew I had some - thing spe - cial with you. But
all a - long, I knew I had some - thing spe - cial with you. But

Em
G
some - times _ you just got - ta know _ that these things _ fall through. But I'm
some - times _ you just got - ta know _ that these things _ fall through. I can't
1
Bm
D
still tired _ and I can't hide my con - nec - tion with you.
2
Bm
hide my con - nec - tion with _ you. _
Bm
G
I will nev - er for - get you, _
3
A
Bm
G
and you'll al - ways be by my side. From the day that I met you, _

A/E
I knew that I would love you till the day I die. And I will nev -
Bm
G
- er want much more, and in my heart I will al - ways be
A
Bm
G
3
sure that I will ne - ver for - get you, and you'll
3
al - ways be by my side till the day I die,
N.C.
Bm
(with ad lib. vocals)
till the day I die,

G
A
Bm
till the day I die,
till the day I die,
till the day I die,
G
Em
till the day I die,
till the day I die.
I will
Bm
G
A
nev - er for - get you,
I will
Bm
G
Em
N.C.
nev - er for - get you,
till the day I die.
3

SOMETHING JUST LIKE THIS

Words and Music by ANDREW TAGGART,
CHRIS MARTIN, GUY BERRYMAN,
JONNY BUCKLAND and WILL CHAMPION

G(add9)
A(add4)
Bm7
go? How much you wan-na risk? I'm not look-ing for some-bod-y with some su-per-hu-man
gifts, some su-per-he-ro, some fair-y-tale bliss. Just some thing I can
To Coda
turn to, some-bod-y I can kiss. I want some-thing just like this. Do do do do do do,
do do do do, do do do do do do. Oh, I want some-thing just like

G(add9)
A(add4)
Bm7
A(add4)
G(add9)
A(add4)
this. Do do do do do do,
do do do do,
do do do do do do.
Bm7
A(add4)
G(add9)
A(add4)
Bm7
A(add4)
Oh, I want some-thing just like this.
G(add9)
A(add4)
Bm7
A(add4)
G(add9)
A(add4)
I want some-thing just like this."
D.S. al Coda
Bm7
A(add4)
G(add9)
A(add4)
Bm7
A(add4)
I've been read-ing books of

CODA
Bm7
A(add4)
G(add9)
A(add4)
Bm7
A(add4)
miss. I want some-thing just like this.
G(add9)
A(add4)
1
Bm7
A(add4)
I want some-thing just like
2
Bm7
A(add4)
Oh, I want some-thing just like
G5
A5
Bm
F♯m7
G5
A5
this. Do do do do do do, do do do do do, do do do do do do.
Bm
F♯m7
G5
A5
Bm
F♯m7
Oh, I want some-thing just like this. Do do do do do do, do do do do,

G5
A5
Bm
F♯m7
G
A
do do do do do do.
Where d'you wan-na go?
How much you wan-na risk?
I'm not look-ing for some-bod-y with some su-per-hu-man gifts,
some su-per-he-ro,
some fair-y-tale bliss.
Just some-thing I can turn to,
some-bod-y I can kiss.
I want some-thing just like this.
Bm7
3fr
5fr

G
D
A
D
A
D/F♯
Asus
Bm
G
D
A
D
A
Oh, I want some-thing just like
this.
G
A
Bm7
F♯m7
G
A
Bm7
F♯m7
G
A
Bm7
F♯m7
G
A

Bm7
F#m7
G
A
Bm7
F#m7
Oh, I want some-thing just like this.
G
A
Bm7
F#m7
G
A
Bm7
F#m7
G(add9)
A(add4)
Bm7
A(add4)
Oh, I want some-thing just like this."
G(add9)
A(add4)
Repeat and Fade
Bm7
A(add4)
Optional Ending
Bm7
A(add4)
G(add9)
rit.

SILENCE

Words and Music by KHALID ROBINSON
and MARSHMELLO

C♯m
E
C♯m
B
Nev-er felt a feel-ing of com - fort, all this time I've been hid - ing. And I
A
E
C♯m
B
nev-er had some-one to call my own, oh, na, I'm so used to shar - ing.
A
E
C♯m
B
Love on - ly left me a - lone, but I'm at one with the si -
A
E
C♯m
B
- lence. I found peace in your vio - lence, can't tell me there's no point in try - ing.
mp

A
E
C♯m
B
4fr
I'm at one and I've been qui-et for too long.
A
E
C♯m
B
4fr
I found peace in your vio - lence, can't tell me there's no point in try - ing.
mf
A
E
C♯m
4fr
N.C.
I'm at one and I've been qui-et for too long.
A
E
C♯m
B
4fr
I've been qui-et for too long.
f

A
E
C♯m
4fr
B
I've been quiet for too long.
I found peace in your violence, can't tell me there's no point in trying.
To Coda
I'm at one and I've been quiet for too long.
I'm in need of a savior, but I'm not asking for favors. My
(savior)

C♯m
E
C♯m
B
whole life, I've felt like a bur - den, I think too much _ and I hate it. I'm
A
E
C♯m
so used to be - ing in the wrong, I'm tired of
B
A
E
car - ing. Lov - ing nev - er gave me _ a home,
C♯m
B
D.S. al Coda
so I'll sit here _ in the si -
CODA
B
long.

SORRY

Words and Music by JUSTIN BIEBER,
SONNY MOORE, MICHAEL TUCKER,
JULIA MICHAELS and JUSTIN TRANTER

B♭
A♭
4fr
pol - o - gies.
I hope I don't run out of
Cm
3fr
B♭
time. Could some - one call the ref - er - ee?
'Cause I just
A♭
4fr
Cm
3fr
B♭
need one more shot at for - give - ness.
A♭
4fr
Cm
3fr
I know you know that I made those mis - takes may - be

B♭
A♭
4fr
once or twice, and by once or twice I mean
Cm
3fr
B♭
may - be a cou - ple a hun - dred times. So,
A♭
4fr
Cm
3fr
B♭
let me, oh, let me re - deem, oh, re - deem, oh, my - self to - night.
A♭
4fr
Cm
3fr
'Cause I just need one more shot at sec - ond chanc -

B♭
A♭(add9)
4fr
- es.
Is it too
Cm7
3fr
late now to say
sor - ry?
'Cause I'm
miss - in' more than just your bod - y.
Oh, oh.
Is it too late now to say

B♭
Fm7
sor - ry?
Yeah, I know,
oh, that I
A♭
B♭
To Coda
let you down. Is it too late to say sor - ry now?
A♭
Cm
B♭
I'm sor - ry,
A♭
Cm
yeah.

B♭
A♭
4fr
Cm
3fr
Sor - ry,
B♭
Fm7
sor - ry. Yeah, I know, oh, that I
A♭
4fr
B♭
let you down. Is it too late to say sor - ry now?
A♭(add9)
4fr
Cm7
3fr
B♭

A♭
4fr
Cm
3fr
B♭
I'll take ev - 'ry sin - gle piece of the blame if you want me to.
But you know that there is no in - no - cent one in this
game for two.
But I'll go, I'll go, and then
you go, you go out and spill the truth.
Can we both

A♭
Cm
B♭
D.S. al Coda
say the words, say for - get this? Yeah,
CODA
I'm not just try'n' to get you back on me,
'cause I'm miss - in' more that just your
bod - y. Oh, oh. Is it too
4fr
3fr

Cm
Bb
late now to say sor - ry?
Yeah, I know
Fm7
Ab
oh, that I let you down. Is it too late to say
Bb
Ab
Cm
Bb
sor - ry now?
I'm sor - ry,
Ab
Cm
Bb
yeah.
Sor - ry,

A♭
Cm
B♭
sor - ry.
Fm7
Yeah, I know, oh, that I let you down. Is
A♭
1
B♭
2
B♭
it too late to say sor - ry now? sor - ry now?
A♭(add9)
Cm7
B♭
A♭(add9)
Cm7
B♭

STAY

Words and Music by ALESSIA CARACCIOLO,
ANDERS FRØEN, JONNALI PARMENIUS,
SARAH AARONS, ANTON ZASLAVSKI
and LINUS WIKLUND

C
Em
D
G
C
Em
D♭
Fm
E♭
A♭
D♭
Fm
hope the winds of change will change your mind.
I could give a thou - sand rea - sons
nev - er been the best at let - ting go.
I don't wan - na spend the night a -
D
C
Em
D
G
E♭
D♭
Fm
E♭
A♭
why.
And I know you,
and you've got to
lone,
guess I need you,
and I need to
C
Em
D
D♭
Fm
E♭
make it on your own, but we don't have to grow up,
we can stay for - ev - er young.
make it on my own, but I don't wan - na grow up,
we can stay for - ev - er young.
C
Em
D
G
D♭
Fm
E♭
A♭
Liv - ing on my so - fa, drink - ing rum and co - la,
un - der - neath the ris - ing sun.
Liv - ing on my so - fa, drink - ing rum and co - la,
un - der - neath the ris - ing sun.

C
Em
D
Db
Fm
Eb
I could give a thou - sand rea - sons why but you're go -
I could give a mil - lion rea - sons why but I'm go -
G
Ab
- ing, and you know that.
- ing, and you know that.
All you have to do is
C(add9)
Em7
Bm6
Db(add9)
Fm7
Cm6
stay a min - ute, just take your time, the clock is tick - ing, so
stay. All you have to do is wait a sec - ond, your hands on mine, the

To Coda
C(add9)
D
Em7
Bm7
D♭(add9)
E♭
Fm7
Cm6
clock is tick-ing, so stay.
(All you have to do is...)
B7
All you have to do is
stay.
C
Em
D
D♭
Fm
All you have to do is
p

C
Em
D
G
C
Em
D♭
Fm
E♭
A♭
D♭
Fm
stay,
so
stay.
D
C
Em
D
E♭
D♭
Fm
E♭
D.S. al Coda
All you have to do is
CODA
Em7
Fm7
C
D♭
Em
Fm
stay.
All you have to do is
stay.
(Mmm,
D
C
Em
D
E♭
D♭
Fm
E♭
mmm,
mmm,
mmm.)

TITANIUM

Words and Music by DAVID GUETTA,
SIA FURLER, GIORGIO TUINFORT
and NIK VAN DE WALL

E♭(add2)
6fr
E♭(add2)/G
I'm talk - ing loud,
not say - ing much.
Mm, ghost town
and haunt - ed love.
Csus
3fr
E♭(add2)
6fr
I'm crit - i - cized,
Raise your voice;
E♭(add2)/D
3fr
Csus
3fr
but all your bul - lets ri - co - chet.
sticks and stones may break my bones...
E♭(add2)
6fr
E♭(add2)/G
You shoot me down,
but I get up.
Talk - ing loud,
not say - ing much.

Csus
3fr
A♭
4fr
I'm bul - let - proof,
B♭
Gm
3fr
Cm
3fr
nothing to lose;
fi - re a - way,
fire a - way.
A♭
4fr
B♭
Gm
3fr
Ri - co - chet;
you take your aim;
fi - re a - way,
Cm
3fr
A♭
4fr
fire a - way.
You shoot me down,

B♭
Gm
Cm
3fr
but I won't fall;
I am ti - ta - ni - um.
A♭
4fr
You shoot me down,
but I won't fall;
I am ti - ta -
- ni - um.
B♭(add2)
1

B♭(add2)
3fr
Gm
3fr
Cm
3fr
2
Gm
Cm
A♭
4fr
I am ti - ta - ni - um.
B♭(add2)
Gm
Cm
I am ti - ta - ni - um.
A♭
B♭
Gm
Cm
Stone - hard; ma - chine gun, fir - ing at the ones who run.

A♭
4fr
B♭
Cm
3fr
Stone - hard,
that was bul - let-proof
glass.
C5
3fr
A♭
4fr
B♭
You shoot me
down,
but I won't fall;
Gm
3fr
Cm
3fr
A♭
4fr
I am ti - ta
- ni
- um.
You shoot me
down,
B♭
Gm
3fr
but I won't fall;
I am ti - ta -

1
2
Cm
A♭
B♭(add2)
Gm
N.C.
3fr
4fr
- ni - um.
You shoot me down,
- ni - um.
I am ti - ta - ni - um.

TAKE ME HOME

Words and Music by SAMUEL FRISCH,
BRANDON LOWRY, ALEX MAKHLOUF,
JEAN PAUL MAKHLOUF and BLETA REXHA

Em7
C
G
Am7
did you turn so cold? You cut me down to the bone; now you're
best mis-take was you. And you're my sweet af-flic-tion 'cause you
Em7
C
G
Am7
danc-in' all o-ver my soul. I'm fall-in' to piec-es, to
hurt me right, but you do it nice. 'Round in cir-cles, here we go,
Em7
C
G
Am7
piec-es, to piec-es.
yeah.
But I still stay 'cause you're the
Em7
D
Csus2
G
Am7
on-ly thing I know. So won't you take, oh,

Em7
D
Csus2
G
won't you take me home? Take me home,
Am7
Em7
C
home, home. Take me
G
Am7
Em7
home, home, home.
C
N.C.
G
Am7(add4)
Take me.

To Coda
Em7
Csus2
G
Take me,
Am7(add4)
Em7
1
Csus2
G
take me,
take me,
take me
home.
2
Csus2
D.S. al Coda
take me
CODA
Csus2
G
Take me
home.
I
still
stay.
Am7(add4)
Em7
Csus2
G
Oh,
won't you take
me home?
Take me
home.

THIS IS WHAT YOU CAME FOR

Words and Music by CALVIN HARRIS
and TAYLOR SWIFT

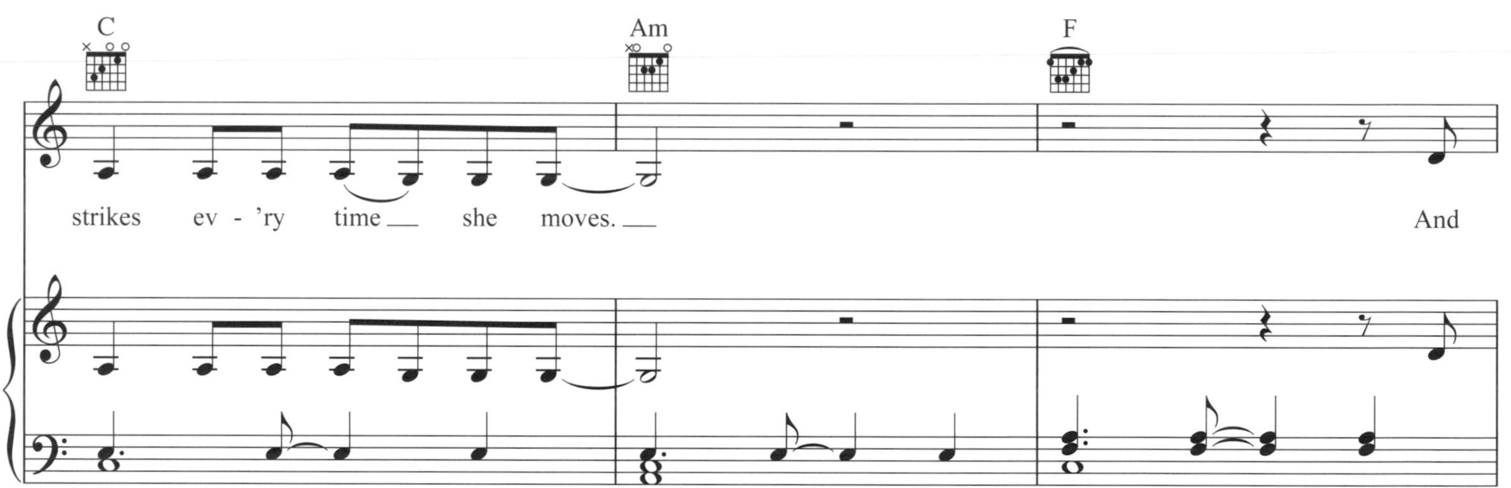

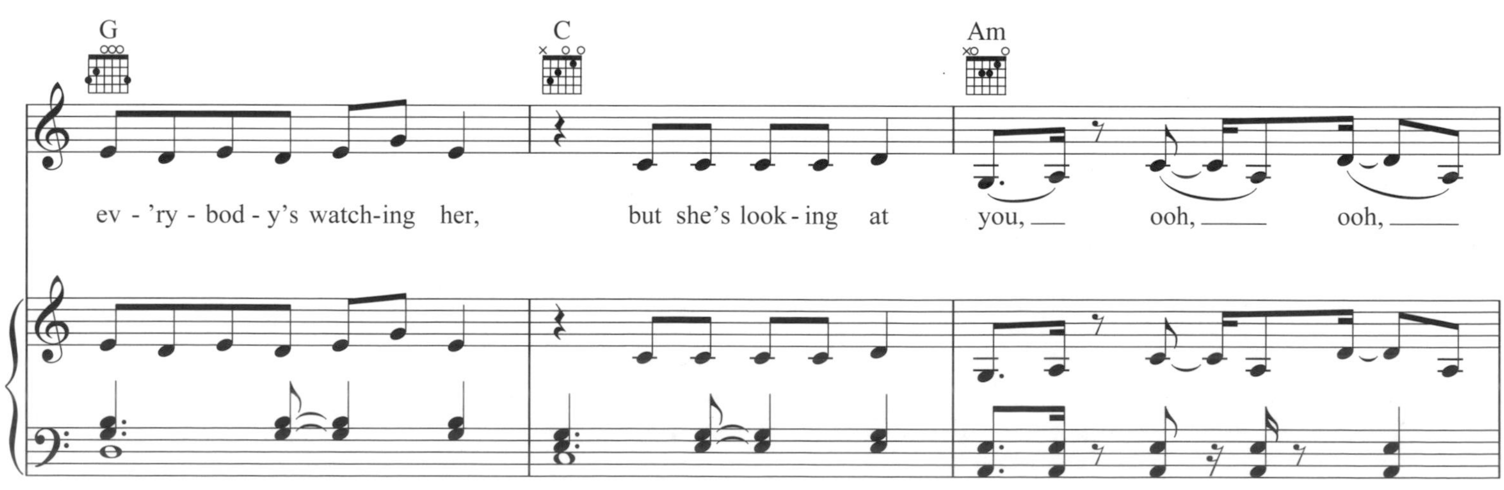

F
G
C
you, ooh, ooh, you, ooh, ooh, you, ooh, ooh,
Am
F
G
you, ooh, ooh, you, ooh, ooh, ooh.
C
Fmaj7
Ba - by, this is what you came for.
G
Am7
Fmaj7
Light - ning strikes ev - 'ry time she moves.

G
Am7
And ev - 'ry - bod - y's watch - ing her, but she's look - ing at
Fmaj7
G
you, ooh, ooh, you, ooh, ooh, you, ooh, ooh,
Am7
Fmaj7
you, ooh, ooh, you, ooh, ooh, you, ooh, ooh,
G
Am7
Fmaj7
ooh. You, ooh, ooh,

G
Am7
you, ooh, ooh, you, ooh, ooh, you, ooh, ooh,
Fmaj7
you, ooh, ooh, you, ooh, ooh,
To Coda
G
Am7
Am
ooh. We go
F/A
G/A
3fr
Am
fast at the game we play.

F/A
G/A
3fr
Who knows why it's got - ta be this way?
Am
F/A
We say noth - ing more than we need.
G/A
3fr
Am7
Am
I say,
F/A
G/A
3fr
Am7
D.S. al Coda
"Your place" when we leave.

CODA
Am7
Am
F
Ba - by, this is what you came for.
G
C
Am
Light - ning strikes ev - 'ry time she moves.
F
G
C
Oh.
Am
Fmaj7/A
G/A
3fr
Ba - by, this is what you came for. Light - ning

Am7
Am
Fmaj7/A
strikes ev - 'ry time she moves.
And
G/A
3fr
Am7
ev - 'ry - bod - y's watch - ing her,
but she's look - ing at
Fmaj7
G
you, ooh, ooh, you, ooh, ooh, you, ooh, ooh,
Am7
Fmaj7
you, ooh, ooh, you, ooh, ooh.

G
Am7
you, ooh, ooh, ooh.
Fmaj7
G
You, ooh, ooh, you, ooh, ooh, you, ooh, ooh,
Am7
Fmaj7
you, ooh, ooh, you, ooh, ooh,
G
Am7
you, ooh, ooh, ooh.

WAKE ME UP

Words and Music by ALOE BLACC,
TIM BERGLING and MICHAEL EINZIGER

Bm
G
D/A
They tell me I'm too young to un - der - stand.
Bm
G
D/A
They say I'm caught up in a dream.
Bm
G
D/A
Well, life will pass me by if I don't o - pen up my eyes.
Bm
G
D/A
Well, that's fine by me.
So wake me

Bm G D A Bm G
up when it's all o - ver, when I'm wis - er and I'm old -
D F#7 Bm G D A
- er. All this time I was find - in' my - self and I
Bm G D F#7 Bm G
did - n't know I was lost. So wake me up when it's all o -
D A Bm G D F#7
- ver, when I'm wis - er and I'm old - er. All this

To Coda
Bm
G
D
A
Bm
G
time I was find - in' my - self
and I
and I,
did - n't know I was
D
Bm
G
D
A
lost.
Bm
G
D
F#7
Bm
G
D
A
Bm
G
N.C.

Bm
G
D
A
Bm
G
D
F♯7
Bm
G
D
A
Bm
G
D
F♯7
Bm
G
I tried car-ry-ing the weight
D/A
Bm
G
D/A
of the world,
but I on - ly have two
hands.

Bm
G
D/A
Bm
G
Hope I get a chance to trav - el the world,
but I don't have an - y plans.
D/A
Bm
G
D
D/A
Wish that I could stay for - ev - er this young.
Bm
G
D
D/A
Bm
G
Not a - fraid to close my eyes.
Life's a game made for
D
Asus
A
Bm
G
D
D.S. al Coda
N.C.
ev - 'ry - one
and love is the prize.
So wake me

CODA
Bm
G
D
F#7
I did - n't know I was lost.
A
Lead vocal ad lib.
End vocal ad lib.

Bm
G
D
F♯7
Bm
G
D
A
Bm
G
N.C.
Bm
G
D
A
Bm
G
D
F♯7
Bm
G
D
A
Bm
G
D
F♯7
Bm

WHERE ARE Ü NOW

Words and Music by SONNY MOORE,
THOMAS PENTZ, JASON BOYD,
KARL RUBIN BRUTUS, JUSTIN BIEBER
and JORDAN WARE

Em
D
G
See I gave you faith, turned your doubt into hop-in'. Can't de-ny
C
Em
D
it. Now I'm all a-lone and my joy's turned to mop-in'.
G
C
C
Em
Tell me where are you now that I need you?
D
G
C
Where are you now? Where are you
3

Em
D
G
now that I need you? Could-n't find you an - y - where.
C
Em
D
When you broke down, I did - n't leave you.
G
C
Em
I was by your side. So, where are you now that I need you?
3
3
D
N.C.
Where are you now that I need you?

Em
G
C
D
Am
Em
G
C
D
Am
Where are you now that I need you?

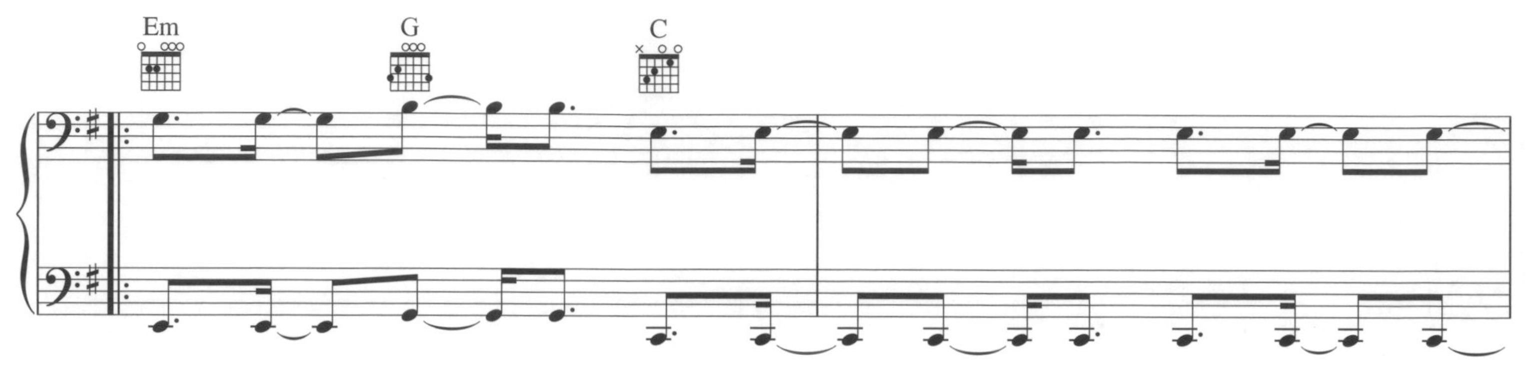
Em
G
C

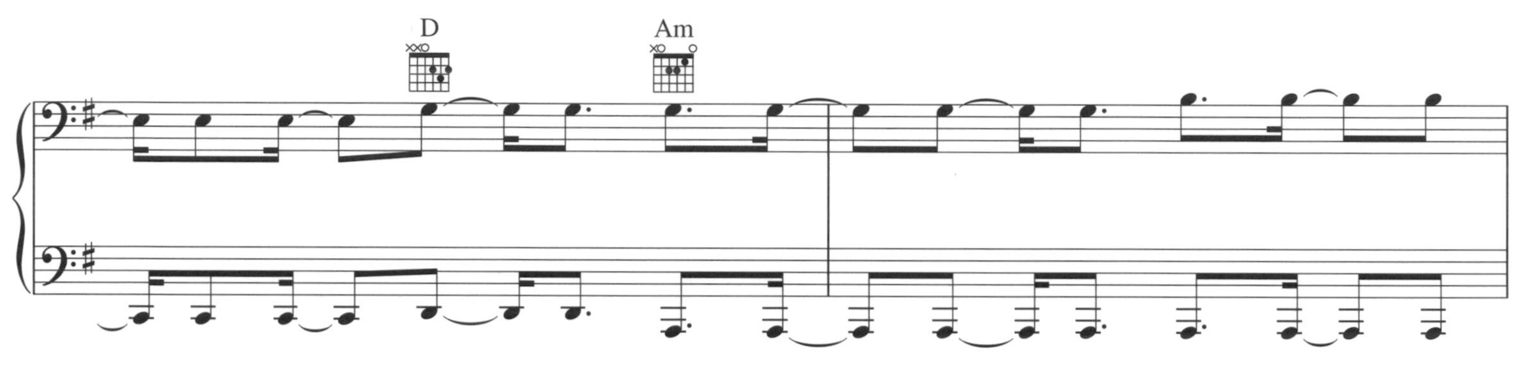
D
Am

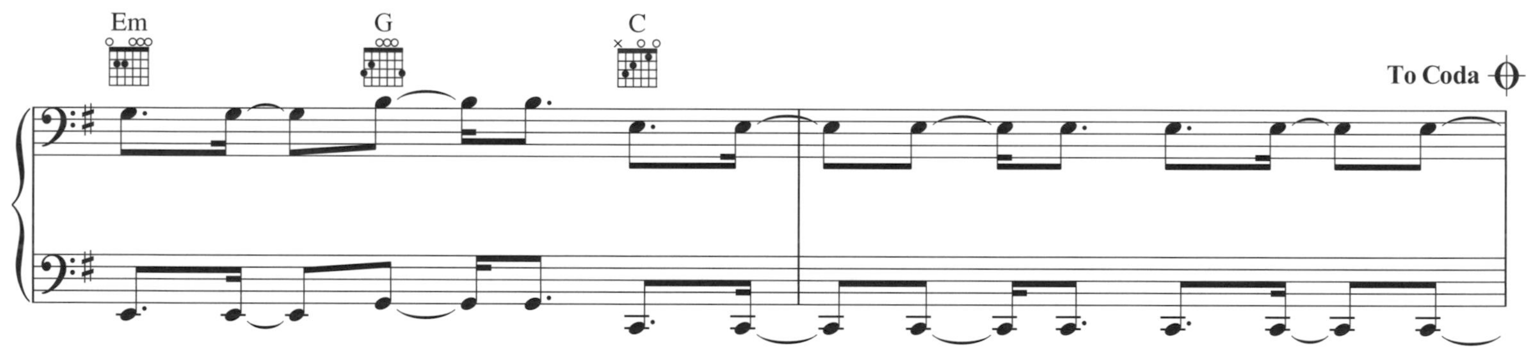
Em
G
C
To Coda

D
Am
Where are you now that I need you?

N.C.
C
Em
I gave you at - ten - tion when no -
D
G
C
bod - y else was pay - in'.
Em
D
G
I gave you the shirt off my back. What you say - in'?
To keep you warm.
C
Em
D
I showed you the game ev - 'ry - bod - y else was play - in'.

G
C
Em
That's for sure.
And I was on my knees when no-
D
G
C
bod-y else was pray-in'.
Oh, Lord.
Em
D
G
C
Where are you now that I need you?

C
Em
D
1
G
C
Where are you now that I need you?
2
N.C.
D.S. al Coda
I need you the most.
CODA
N.C.
I need you the most.

WOLVES

Words and Music by SELENA GOMEZ,
CARL ROSEN, ANDREW WOTMAN,
ALI TAMPOSI, LOUIS BELL
and MARSHMELLO

D(add2)
Gmaj7
Asus
that we did that sum - mer night,
night,
Bm
D(add2)
Gmaj7
drunk on a feel - ing, a - lone with the stars in the sky.
G
A
I been run-ning through the jun - gle, I been run-ning with the wolves to get to
Bm
A
G
you, to get to you.
I been down the dark - est al - leys, saw the

A
Bm
D
dark side of the moon to get to you, _ to get to you. _ I looked for
Gmaj7
A
Bm
love in ev - 'ry stran-ger, took too much to ease the an - ger, all for you, _ yeah, all for
A
G
A
you. I been run-ning through the jun - gle, I been cry-ing with the wolves to get to
Bm
N.C.
G
you, _ to get to you, to get to you. (Ah,

A
Bm
Dmaj7
G
ah,
ah,
ah,
to get to
you.
Ah,
A
Bm
1
Dmaj7
Bm
ah,
ah,
ah,
to get to
you.)
Your fin-ger-tips
2
D
G
A
I been
run-ning through the jun-gle,
I been
run-ning
with
the wolves to
get
to
ah,
to
get
to
you.)
Bm
A
G
you,
to
get
to
you.
I
been
down
the dark - est
al - leys,
saw
the

A
Bm
D
dark side of the moon to get to you, to get to you. I looked for
G
A
Bm
love in ev - 'ry stran - ger, took too much to ease the an - ger, all for you, yeah, all for
A
G
A
you. I been run-ning through the jun - gle, I been cry-ing with the wolves to get to
Bm
D
N.C.
you, to get to you, to get to you.

2U

Words and Music by JUSTIN BIEBER,
DAVID GUETTA, JASON BOYD,
GIORGIO TUINFORT and DANIEL TUPARIA

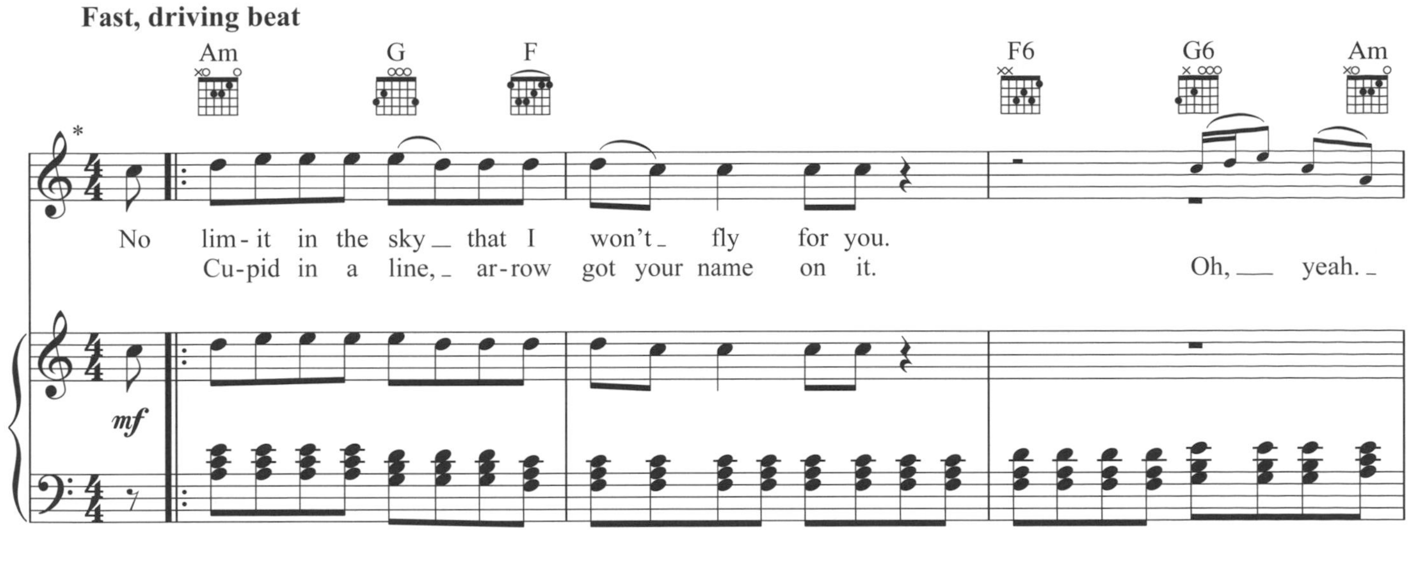

* *Recorded a half step lower.*

G/A
Am
3fr
I want you to share that air with me.
There's no prom-
ain't got-ta wake up to an emp-ty bed.
Share my life;
G
F
Dm
G
Am
ise that I won't keep.
I'll climb a moun-tain; there's none too steep.
it's yours to keep,
now that I give to you all of me.
C
G
F
When it comes to you,
Dm
G
Em
there's no crime.
Let's take both of our

Am
Dm
F
G
souls _ and in - ter - twine. When it
C
G
F
Dm
comes to you, don't be
G
Em
Am
blind. Watch me speak from _ my heart when _ it
F/A
G/A
3fr
Am
F/A
G/A
3fr
To Coda
comes to you, comes to

Am Am G6

you.

F G

Am G Am Cmaj7 F

Want you _ to share that.

1

G Am N.C.

When it comes to you.

2
G
N.C.
Am
G
F
When it comes to you.
G
Am
N.C.
Want you to share that.
Am
Cmaj7
F
G
Am
D.S. al Coda
G
When it
CODA
Am
you.

YOU KNOW YOU LIKE IT

Words and Music by WILLIAM SAMI GRIGAHCINE,
STEVE GUESS, ALUNA DEWJI-FRANCIS
and GEORGE REID

Moderate Dance Pop

py not tip - ping the scales. I just won't play,
be so damn cruel. Ba - by, you got
let - tin' my life get a - way.
noth - ing to prove.
A♭
Fm
I'm no fool, no.
Cm
B♭
A♭
Fm
I'm not a fol - low - er. I don't take things as they come
Cm
B♭
A♭
Fm
if they bring me down. Life can be cruel

Cm
B♭
A♭
Fm
3fr
4fr
if ___ you're a dream - er. ___
I just wan - na have some fun.
Don't tell me what could be done.
You know you like it, but it drives you in - sane.
You know you like it, but it drives you in - sane. _
You know you like it, but you're scared of the shame.
What you want? What you gon - na do?
You know you like it, but it drives you in - sane.

Cm
Bb
Ab
Fm
Fol-low me 'cause you know that you wan-na feel the same.
You know you like it, but it drives you in-sane.
N.C.
What you want? What you gon-na do?
Da, da, da, da, da, da,
da, da, da, da, (drives you in - sane.)
Da, da, da, da, da, da, da.
Da, da, da, da, da, da,

Cm
B♭
A♭
Fm
da, da, da, da, (drives you in - sane.)
Cm
B♭
1
N.C.
Da, da, da, da, da, da, da. If you wan - na train me
2
A♭
Fm
Cm
B♭
A♭
Fm
(Drives you in - sane.)
Cm
B♭
A♭
Fm

Cm
B♭
A♭
Fm
N.C.
(Drives you in - sane, ah.)
A♭
Fm
Cm
B♭
A♭
Fm
Da, da, da, da, da, da, da, da, da, da, (drives you in - sane.)
Play 4 times
Cm
B♭
A♭
Fm7
Cm
B♭6
Da, da, da, da, da, da, da.
A♭
Fm7
1
Cm
B♭6
2
Cm

THE NEW DECADE SERIES

Books with Online Audio • Arranged for Piano, Voice, and Guitar

The New Decade Series features collections of iconic songs from each decade with great backing tracks so you can play them and sound like a pro. You access the tracks online for streaming or download. **See complete song listings online at www.halleonard.com**

SONGS OF THE 1920s

Ain't Misbehavin' • Baby Face • California, Here I Come • Fascinating Rhythm • I Wanna Be Loved by You • It Had to Be You • Mack the Knife • Ol' Man River • Puttin' on the Ritz • Rhapsody in Blue • Someone to Watch over Me • Tea for Two • Who's Sorry Now • and more.

00137576 P/V/G................................$24.99

SONGS OF THE 1930s

As Time Goes By • Blue Moon • Cheek to Cheek • Embraceable You • A Fine Romance • Georgia on My Mind • I Only Have Eyes for You • The Lady Is a Tramp • On the Sunny Side of the Street • Over the Rainbow • Pennies from Heaven • Stormy Weather (Keeps Rainin' All the Time) • The Way You Look Tonight • and more.

00137579 P/V/G................................$24.99

SONGS OF THE 1940s

At Last • Boogie Woogie Bugle Boy • Don't Get Around Much Anymore • God Bless' the Child • How High the Moon • It Could Happen to You • La Vie En Rose (Take Me to Your Heart Again) • Route 66 • Sentimental Journey • The Trolley Song • You'd Be So Nice to Come Home To • Zip-A-Dee-Doo-Dah • and more.

00137582 P/V/G................................$24.99

SONGS OF THE 1950s

Ain't That a Shame • Be-Bop-A-Lula • Chantilly Lace • Earth Angel • Fever • Great Balls of Fire • Love Me Tender • Mona Lisa • Peggy Sue • Que Sera, Sera (Whatever Will Be, Will Be) • Rock Around the Clock • Sixteen Tons • A Teenager in Love • That'll Be the Day • Unchained Melody • Volare • You Send Me • Your Cheatin' Heart • and more.

00137595 P/V/G................................$24.99

SONGS OF THE 1960s

All You Need Is Love • Beyond the Sea • Born to Be Wild • California Girls • Dancing in the Street • Happy Together • King of the Road • Leaving on a Jet Plane • Louie, Louie • My Generation • Oh, Pretty Woman • Sunshine of Your Love • Under the Boardwalk • You Really Got Me • and more.

00137596 P/V/G................................$24.99

SONGS OF THE 1970s

ABC • Bridge over Troubled Water • Cat's in the Cradle • Dancing Queen • Free Bird • Goodbye Yellow Brick Road • Hotel California • I Will Survive • Joy to the World • Killing Me Softly with His Song • Layla • Let It Be • Piano Man • The Rainbow Connection • Stairway to Heaven • The Way We Were • Your Song • and more.

00137599 P/V/G................................$27.99

SONGS OF THE 1980s

Addicted to Love • Beat It • Careless Whisper • Come on Eileen • Don't Stop Believin' • Every Rose Has Its Thorn • Footloose • I Just Called to Say I Love You • Jessie's Girl • Livin' on a Prayer • Saving All My Love for You • Take on Me • Up Where We Belong • The Wind Beneath My Wings • and more.

00137600 P/V/G................................$27.99

SONGS OF THE 1990s

Angel • Black Velvet • Can You Feel the Love Tonight • (Everything I Do) I Do It for You • Friends in Low Places • Hero • I Will Always Love You • More Than Words • My Heart Will Go On (Love Theme from 'Titanic') • Smells like Teen Spirit • Under the Bridge • Vision of Love • Wonderwall • and more.

00137601 P/V/G................................$27.99

SONGS OF THE 2000s

Bad Day • Beautiful • Before He Cheats • Chasing Cars • Chasing Pavements • Drops of Jupiter (Tell Me) • Fireflies • Hey There Delilah • How to Save a Life • I Gotta Feeling • I'm Yours • Just Dance • Love Story • 100 Years • Rehab • Unwritten • You Raise Me Up • and more.

00137608 P/V/G................................$27.99

SONGS OF THE 2010s

All About That Bass • All of Me • Brave • Empire State of Mind • Get Lucky • Happy • Hey, Soul Sister • I Knew You Were Trouble • Just the Way You Are • Need You Now • Pompeii • Radioactive • Rolling in the Deep • Shake It Off • Shut up and Dance • Stay with Me • Take Me to Church • Thinking Out Loud • Uptown Funk • and many more.

00151836 P/V/G................................$27.99

halleonard.com

Prices, content, and availability subject to change without notice.